FIFTY MAJOR DOCUMENTS OF THE TWENTIETH CENTURY
1950–2000

by
Taylor Stults

AN ANVIL ORIGINAL
Under the general editorship of
Hans L. Trefousse

KRIEGER PUBLISHING COMPANY
MALABAR, FLORIDA
2004

Original Edition 2004

Printed and Published by
KRIEGER PUBLISHING COMPANY
KRIEGER DRIVE
MALABAR, FLORIDA 32950

Copyright © 2004 by Taylor Stults

Library of Congress Cataloging-in-Publication Data

Fifty major documents of the twentieth century, 1950–2000 / [edited by] Taylor Stults.
   p. cm.
  ISBN 1-57524-204-4 (pbk. : alk. paper)
    1. Europe—History—1945—Sources. 2. World politics—1945—Sources.
  3. History, Modern—1945–1989—Sources. 4. Cold War—Sources. I. Title:
  50 major documents of the twentieth century, 1950–2000. II. Stults, Taylor, 1936–

D839.3.F55   2004
909.82′5—dc21   2002043376

10 9 8 7 6 5 4 3 2

For Jan

THE ANVIL SERIES

Anvil paperbacks give an original analysis of a major field of history or a problem area, drawing upon the most recent research. They present a concise treatment and can act as supplementary material for college history courses. Written by many of the outstanding historians in the United States, the format is one-half narrative text, one-half supporting documents, often from hard to find sources.

This particular volume is an exception to the usual format in that it contains only documents, although each one is preceded by a paragraph or two of background information. These documents relate to significant events of the second half of the twentieth century. It is a followup to the previous Anvil, Louis L. Snyder's *Fifty Major Documents of the Twentieth Century*. Dr. Snyder's book covers the first half of the twentieth century.

CONTENTS

Preface   vii

1. A Western View of the Soviet Union, 1950	1
2. The European Coal and Steel Community, 1951	2
3. The European Defense Community, 1952	5
4. West Germany Joins NATO, 1954	10
5. The Geneva Conference, 1955	12
6. The Warsaw Pact, 1955	14
7. Khrushchev's Anti-Stalin Speech, 1956	18
8. British Policy in the Suez Crisis, 1956	25
9. U.S. Policy During the Suez Crisis, 1956	29
10. Soviet Policy in Hungary, 1956	35
11. Imre Nagy's Final Message, 1956	37
12. The Common Market, 1957	38
13. Boris Pasternak and the Zhivago Controversy, 1956–1958	41
14. De Gaulle Takes Power in France, 1958	46
15. The Berlin Crisis, 1958	48
16. The Communist Party Program, 1961	52
17. United States Statement on Berlin, 1961	56
18. The Soviet Position on Germany and West Berlin, 1961	58
19. The "Jupiter" Missiles Deal, 1962	64
20. The Cuban Missile Crisis—The Soviet View, 1962	66
21. The American View of the Cuba Situation, 1962	70
22. De Gaulle on France and the United States, 1963	73
23. John Kennedy's Speech in Berlin, 1963	78
24. The Nuclear Test Ban Treaty, 1963	80
25. The Gulf of Tonkin Resolution, 1964	82
26. U.S. Policy in the "Six-Day War," 1967	84
27. President Johnson on Vietnam, 1968	86
28. French Student Demands, 1968	92
29. The Nuclear Non-Proliferation Treaty, 1968	97

30. The "Brezhnev Doctrine," 1968   100
31. Nobel Peace Prize for Willy Brandt, 1971   104
32. The ABM Treaty, 1972   108
33. The Interim Agreement (SALT I), 1972   113
34. The Helsinki Accords, 1975   115
35. Reagan and the "Evil Empire," 1983   119
36. The INF Treaty, 1987   123
37. Anti-Gorbachev Resolution, 1990   128
38. The Conventional Armed Forces Treaty, 1990   130
39. Gorbachev Defends Perestroika, 1991   135
40. The Maastricht Treaty, 1992   140
41. The Partnership for Peace, 1994   146
42. The Dayton Peace Agreement, 1995   151
43. The NATO-Russia Founding Act, 1997   156
44. Havel on the Post-Communist Era, 1997   161
45. NATO Adds New Members, 1997–1999   164
46. NATO Acts Against Yugoslavia, 1999   170
47. Boris Yeltsin's Resignation, 1999   174
48. Germany and the Holocaust, 2000   176
49. The Euro: A New European Currency, 2000   179
50. Charter of Fundamental Rights of the European Union,
    2000   185

About the Author   195

PREFACE

This compilation of documents is intended to be a helpful resource for students in courses dealing with contemporary Europe, international relations, and the Cold War. General readers interested in contemporary world history also should find it useful. Reading the actual documents provides the opportunity to understand more fully the decisions of government leaders, the background behind their actions, and the framework of future behavior.

This collection covers the years from 1950 through 2000. Many of the documents trace the Cold War and its end by the latter part of the century. It also includes materials showing the efforts of European states to cooperate more closely in their economic and political relations. An introduction has been provided for each document to give background and context.

A useful resource in the Anvil series for the first half of the twentieth century is Louis L. Snyder's *Fifty Major Documents of the Twentieth Century*, published in the 1950s. As a college instructor teaching twentieth-century European history for over three decades, I found his paperback to be an excellent supplement for my students. Now, with the passage of time and the events of recent decades, it is appropriate to provide this sequel to deal with the second half of the century.

Taylor Stults

DOCUMENT NO. 1

A WESTERN VIEW OF THE SOVIET UNION, 1950*

By 1950, the "Cold War" between the United States and the Soviet Union was increasingly confrontational. Eastern Europe had fallen under communist control, the division of Germany between communist and non-communist regions was complete, and the arms race intensified after Moscow successfully detonated its first atomic bomb in 1949. The Western democracies established the North Atlantic Treaty Organization (NATO) in 1949 as a defensive response against further Soviet expansion into Central and Western Europe. In Asia, the communists under Mao Tse Tung (Mao Zedong) seized power in China in 1949 after a devastating civil war. The spread of communism convinced the West that it must be resisted, even if involving possible military conflict. The following is a message to the U.S. Secretary of State from the American ambassador in the Soviet Union, Alan G. Kirk. His analysis of the East–West relationship and negative characterization of Soviet leaders conveys the atmosphere of this dangerous period in world affairs. Vishinsky was Soviet Foreign Minister, Chou En-lai (Zhou Enlai) the Chinese Foreign Minister, and Malenkov a senior member of the Communist leadership in Moscow. The abbreviated grammatical style in Kirk's dispatch further illustrates the urgency of his message.

γ   γ   γ

SECRET

Moscow, January 24, 1950—6 p.m.

Vishinsky's reply to Secretary of State . . . indicates by its violence that a sensitive spot was hit hard but extreme insolence of language is one more symptom of way in which Soviets are becoming increasingly rash as they seemingly think their position strengthens and ours weakens. If [U.S.] Embassy correctly reading signs, as long as this trend continues we may expect more and more rough treatment, less and less respect for common courtesies or for American public opinion.

* Foreign Relations of the United States, 1950: Central and Eastern Europe; the Soviet Union (Washington, 1980), IV, pp. 1083–84.

This is not merely conceit of bumpkin risen to power, who rejoices in offending because he thinks he is at last in position to do so with impunity; it is part of later phases of 90-degree turn Stalin has presumably planned for years, ever since that threat of Nazism forced him into alliance with Western democracies: Once he got Germany and Japan safely out of picture he swung ever more sharply away toward his original direction of world revolution based on USSR; in first years it was worth-while not to drop all veils at once, in order to confuse free world and delay its reaction; recently, however, veils have been dropped more and more, and Soviet press now speaks frankly of revolution, which testifies to Stalin's belief that with China won and an economic crisis believed under way he no longer need placate US or try to mask his intentions, but rather has more to gain now by driving straight for his real goal.

This new rashness was reflected in Stalin birthday articles, Soviet press New Year editorials, Malenkov's November 6 speech, etc., and it has also been expressed in action, e.g. in treatment of our officials and other citizens in China, Hungary, Bulgaria, Czechoslovakia; in recent threats of Chou En-lai against French; in Chinese seizure of US, French and Dutch property, and Chinese attitude to recognition by Western Powers and even by India. UN walkout, though hardly deserving to be called rash, nevertheless fits in larger picture.

DOCUMENT NO. 2

THE EUROPEAN COAL AND STEEL COMMUNITY, 1951*

Post–World War II Europe faced the challenge of rebuilding areas devastated by the war. Governments also faced the task of reestablishing foreign trade relationships that had been weakened or destroyed by that conflict. One way to achieve economic stability and strength was cooperating to reduce tariffs and other impediments to trade. One of the earliest examples of this approach was the European Coal and Steel Community, negotiated by the governments of six states: Belgium, France, Italy, Luxembourg, the Nether-

* U.S. Department of State, *American Foreign Policy, 1950–1955: Basic Documents* (Washington, 1957), I, pp. 1039–41.

lands, and West Germany. These nations signed the treaty on April 18, 1951. As its name signifies, the special relationship focused on commodities related to heavy industry. The ECSC proved successful, and the six parties to the treaty negotiated a more extensive agreement on a wider range of commodities and economic relationships. The Treaty of Rome was signed in 1957 to establish the European Economic Community (more commonly known as the "Common Market").

γ   γ   γ

[The governments of Belgium, France, Italy, Luxembourg, the Netherlands, and West Germany],

Considering that world peace may be safeguarded only by creative efforts equal to the dangers which menace it;

Convinced that the contribution which an organized and vital Europe can bring to civilization is indispensable to the maintenance of peaceful relations;

Conscious of the fact that Europe can be built only by concrete actions which create a real solidarity and by the establishment of common bases for economic development;

Desirous of assisting through the expansion of their basic production in raising the standard of living and in furthering the works of peace;

Resolve to substitute for historic rivalries a fusion of their essential interests; to establish, by creating an economic community, the foundation of a broad and independent community among peoples long divided by bloody conflicts; and to lay the bases of institutions capable of giving direction to their future common destiny;

Have decided to create a European Coal and Steel Community. . . .

Article 1

By the present Treaty the High Contracting Parties institute among themselves a European Coal and Steel Community, based on a common market, common objectives, and common institutions.

Article 2

The mission of the European Coal and Steel Community is to contribute to economic expansion, the development of employment and the improvement of the standard of living in the participating countries through the institution, in harmony with the general economy of the member States, of a common market as defined in Article 4. The Community must progressively establish conditions which will in themselves assure the most rational distribution of production at the highest possible level of productivity, while safeguarding the continuity of employment and avoiding the creation of fundamental and persistent disturbances in the economies of the member States.

Article 3

Within the framework of their respective powers and responsibilities and in the common interest, the institutions of the Community shall:

(a) see that the common market is regularly supplied, taking account of the needs of third countries;

(b) assure to all consumers in comparable positions within the common market equal access to the sources of production;

(c) seek the establishment of the lowest prices which are possible without requiring any corresponding rise either in the prices charged by the same enterprises in other transactions or in the price-level as a whole in another period, while at the same time permitting necessary amortization and providing normal possibilities of remuneration for capital invested;

(d) see that conditions are maintained which will encourage enterprises to expand and improve their ability to produce and to promote a policy of rational development of natural resources, avoiding inconsiderate exhaustion of such resources;

(e) promote the improvement of the living and working conditions of the labor force in each of the industries under its jurisdiction so as to make possible the equalization of such conditions in an upward direction;

(f) further the development of international trade and see that equitable limits are observed in prices charged on external markets;

(g) promote the regular expansion and the modernization of production as well as the improvement of its quality, under conditions which preclude any protection against competing industries except where justified by illegitimate action on the part of such industries or in their favor.

Article 4

The following are recognized to be incompatible with the common market for coal and steel, and are, therefore, abolished and prohibited within the Community in the manner set forth in the present Treaty:

(a) import and export duties, or charges with an equivalent effect, and quantitative restrictions on the movement of coal and steel;

(b) measures or practices discriminating among producers, among buyers or among consumers, especially as concerns prices, delivery terms and transportation rates, as well as measures or practices which hamper the buyer in the free choice of his supplier;

(c) subsidies or state assistance, or special charges imposed by the state, in any form whatsoever;

(d) restrictive practices tending towards the division of markets or the exploitation of the consumer. . . .

DOCUMENT NO. 3

THE EUROPEAN DEFENSE COMMUNITY, 1952*

Following the creation of the North Atlantic Treaty Organization (NATO) in 1949, additional steps sought to further strengthen the defense coalition in Western Europe against possible Soviet attack. This led to negotiations for the European Defense Community (EDC), intended to develop a military system that tightly integrated the forces and resources of the EDC members. It also envisaged the creation of a military role for West Germany as a member of an enhanced Western defense effort, the first time since World War II that a military force would be permitted in that country. Six governments negotiated the EDC, including five members of NATO: Belgium, France, Italy, Luxembourg, and the Netherlands, plus West Germany. The treaty was signed on May 27, 1952. But apprehension in the French parliament about the creation of a new West German army played a role in the National Assembly's negative decision on August 30, 1954 to ratify the treaty. As a consequence, the EDC never took effect. The following document contains key portions of the EDC treaty as originally signed in May 1952.

γ   γ   γ

[The governments of Belgium, France, Italy, Luxembourg, the Netherlands, and West Germany], Resolved to contribute to the maintenance of peace, particularly by ensuring the defense of Western Europe against any aggression in cooperation with the free nations, in the spirit of the United Nations Charter, and in close liaison with organizations having the same purpose;

* U.S. Department of State, *American Foreign Policy, 1950–1955* (Washington, 1957), I, pp. 1107–13.

Considering that as complete an integration as possible, compatible with military requirements, of the human and material elements gathered in their Defense Forces within a supranational European organization is the most appropriate means of reaching this goal with all the necessary rapidity and effectiveness;

Certain that such integration will result in the most rational and economic utilization of the resources of their countries, as a result, particularly, of the establishment of a common budget and of common armament programs;

Determined to ensure in this way the development of their military power without prejudicing social progress;

Desirous to safeguard the spiritual and moral values which are the common heritage of their peoples, and convinced that within a common army constituted without discrimination, among the participating States national patriotisms, far from being weakened, can only become consolidated and reconciled in a broader framework;

Conscious that they are thus taking a new and essential step on the road to the formation of a united Europe;

Have decided to create a European Defense Community. . . .

Article 1

By the present Treaty the High Contracting Parties institute among themselves a European Defense Community, supranational in character, consisting of common institutions, common armed Forces and a common budget.

Article 2

1. The objectives of the Community shall be exclusively defensive.

2. Consequently, under the conditions provided for in the present Treaty, it shall ensure the security of the member States against any aggression by participating in Western Defense within the framework of the North Atlantic Treaty and by accomplishing the integration of the defense forces of the member States and the rational and economic utilization of their resources.

3. Any armed aggression directed against any one of the member States in Europe or against the European Defense Forces shall be considered as an attack directed against all of the member States. The member States and the European Defense Forces shall furnish to the State or Forces attacked all military and other aid and assistance in their power.

Article 3

The Community shall accomplish the goals assigned to it by employing the least burdensome and most efficient methods. It shall intervene only to the extent necessary for the fulfillment of its mission and with due respect to public liberties and the fundamental rights of the individual. It shall see to it that the proper interests of member States are taken into consideration to the full extent compatible with its own essential interests.

2. In order to enable the Community to accomplish its mission, the member States shall place at its disposal appropriate contributions determined under the provisions of Articles 87 and 94 below [dealing with budgets and member State contributions to the EDC].

Article 4

The Community shall pursue its action in cooperation with the free nations and with all organizations whose goals are the same as that of the Community.

Article 5

The Community shall cooperate closely with the North Atlantic Treaty Organization.

Article 6

The present Treaty does not involve any discrimination among the member States. . . .

Article 8

1. The institutions of the Community shall be: a Council of Ministers, hereinafter called the Council; a Common Assembly, hereinafter called the Assembly; a Commissariat of the European Defense Community, hereinafter called the Commissariat. . . .

Article 9

The Armed Forces of the Community, hereinafter called "European Defense Forces" shall be composed of contingents placed at the disposal of the Community by the member states with a view to their fusion under the conditions provided for in the present Treaty. No member State shall recruit or maintain national armed forces aside from those provided for in Article 10 below.

Article 10

1. The member States may recruit and maintain national armed forces intended for use in the non-European territories with respect to which they assume defense responsibilities, as well as units stationed in their countries which are required for the maintenance of these forces and for their relief.

2. The member States may also recruit and maintain national armed forces required for international missions assumed by them in Berlin, in Austria or by virtue of a decision of the United Nations. At the termination of these missions, these troops shall be either disbanded or placed at the disposal of the Community. Relief for these troops may be effected, with the consent of the competent Supreme Commander responsible to the North Atlantic Treaty Organization, by exchange with units composed of contingents originating from the member States in question which belong to the European Defense Forces.

3. In each member State elements intended as a bodyguard for the Chief of State shall remain national.

4. The member States may dispose of national naval Forces, on the one hand for the protection of non-European territories for which they assume defense responsibilities as mentioned in Section 1 of this Article and for the protection of communications with and among such territories, and on the other hand to fulfill the obligations falling to them as a result of assumption by them of international missions in Section 2 of this Article or as a result of agreements entered into within the framework of the North Atlantic Treaty prior to the entry into effect of the present Treaty.

5. The total volume of national armed forces provided for in this Article, including support units, shall not be so great as to compromise the participation of each member State in the European Defense Forces as determined by agreement among the Governments of the member States. The member States shall have the right to exchange individual personnel between the contingents placed by them at the disposal of the European Defense Forces and the forces which are not a part thereof, provided no diminution in the European Defense Forces occurs as a result.

Article 11

Police forces and forces of gendarmerie, suitable exclusively for the maintenance of internal order, may be recruited and maintained on the territories of the member States. The national character of these forces is not affected by the present Treaty. The volume and nature of such forces existing on the territories of member States shall be such as not to exceed the limits imposed by their mission.

Article 12

1. In case of disturbances or threatened disturbances within the territory of a member State in Europe, such part of the contingents supplied by such State to the European Defense Forces as is necessary to meet the situation shall, on its request, the Council having been informed, be placed at its disposal by the Commissariat. The conditions under which these elements may be employed shall be determined by the legislation in force in the territory of the member States making the request.

2. In case of disaster or calamity requiring immediate aid, elements of the European Defense Forces, which are in a position to be of use, shall give their aid without regard to their national origin. . . .

Article 15

1. The European Defense Forces shall consist of conscripted personnel and of professional personnel serving for a long term by voluntary enlistment.

2. The European Defense Forces shall be integrated in accordance with the organic provisions of Article 68, 69 and 70 [army, air force, navy]. . . . They shall wear a common uniform. They shall be organized according to types defined in the Military Protocol. Such organization may be modified by unanimous decision of the Council.

3. The contingents destined to make up the units of the European Defense Forces shall be furnished by the member States in accordance with a plan to be established by agreement among the Governments concerned. This plan may be revised in accordance with the provisions of Article 44 [military personnel]. . . .

Article 16

The internal defense of the territories of the member States against attacks of any nature having military ends and provoked or carried out by an external enemy shall be ensured by homogeneous formations of European status, which shall be specialists in each country in accordance with the particular defense mission required by its territory, and the operational command of which shall be exercised as provided in Article 18 below.

Article 17

The protection of the civilian population (civil defense) shall be ensured by each of the member States.

Article 18

1. The competent Supreme Commander responsible to the North Atlantic Treaty Organization shall, except as provided in Section 3 of this Article, be empowered to satisfy himself that the European Defense Forces are organized, equipped, trained and prepared for use in a satisfactory manner. . . .

2. During wartime, the competent Supreme Commander of the North Atlantic Treaty Organization shall exercise with regard to the Forces provided for above the full powers and responsibilities of Supreme Commander, such as these are conferred upon him by his terms of reference.

3. In the case of units of the European Defense Forces assigned to internal defense and to the protection of the maritime approaches to the territories of the member States, the authorities which shall command and employ such units shall be determined either by North Atlantic Treaty Organization conventions concluded within the framework of the North Atlantic Treaty or by agreements between the North Atlantic Treaty Organization and the Community.

4. If the North Atlantic Treaty should cease to be in effect before the present Treaty, the member States shall, by agreement among themselves, decide upon the authority to which the command and employment of the European Defense Forces shall be entrusted. . . .

DOCUMENT NO. 4

WEST GERMANY JOINS NATO, 1954*

The Cold War between the Western democracies and the Soviet Union became more elaborate as the two rivals maneuvered to hold their positions and also support their regional European allies. The division of Germany into two separate states, one democratic and one communist, illustrated the confrontational atmosphere in central Europe. The important geographic and strategic position of West Germany encouraged NATO (North Atlantic

* U.S. Department of State, *American Foreign Policy, 1950–1955* (Washington, 1957), I, pp. 871–873.

Treaty Organization) to favor its entry into the Western alliance. French concerns over a rearmed Germany had to be resolved, and assurances were given Paris on the creation of a West German military. The following protocol to the North Atlantic Treaty, signed on October 23, 1954, took effect in 1955 when West Germany became the fifteenth member of the alliance.

γ   γ   γ

The Parties to the North Atlantic Treaty signed at Washington on 4th April 1949,

Being satisfied that the security of the North Atlantic area will be enhanced by the accession of the Federal Republic of Germany to that Treaty, and

Having noted that the Federal Republic of Germany has by a declaration dated 3rd October, 1954, accepted the obligations set forth in Article 2 of the Charter of the United Nations and has undertaken upon its accession to the North Atlantic Treaty from any action inconsistent with the strictly defensive character of that Treaty, and

Having further noted that all member governments have associated themselves with the declaration also made on 3rd October, 1954, by the Governments of the United States of America, the United Kingdom of Great Britain and Northern Ireland and the French Republic in connection with the aforesaid declaration of the Federal Republic of Germany,

Agreed as follows:

Article 1

Upon the entry into force of the present Protocol, the Government of the United States of America shall on behalf of the Parties communicate to the Government of the Federal Republic of Germany an invitation to accede to the North Atlantic Treaty. Thereafter the Federal Republic of Germany shall become a Party to that Treaty on the date when it deposits its instruments of accession with the Government of the United States of America in accordance with Article 10 of that Treaty.

Article II

The present Protocol shall enter into force, when (a) each of the Parties to the North Atlantic Treaty has notified . . . the Government of the United States of America its acceptance thereof, (b) all instruments of ratification of the Protocol Modifying and Completing the Brussels Treaty have been deposited with the Belgian Government, and (c) all instruments of ratification or approval of the Convention on the Presence of Foreign Forces in the Federal Republic of Germany have been deposited with the Government of the Federal Republic of Germany. The Government of the United States of America shall inform the other Parties to the North Atlantic Treaty of the date of the receipt of each notification of acceptance of the present Protocol and of the date of the entry into force of the present Protocol.

Article III

The present Protocol, of which the English and French texts are equally authentic, shall be deposited in the archives of the Government of the United States of America. Duly certified copies thereof shall be transmitted by that Government to the Governments of the other Parties to the North Atlantic Treaty. . . . Signed at Paris the twenty-third day of October nineteen hundred and fifty four. . . .

DOCUMENT NO. 5

THE GENEVA CONFERENCE, 1955*

The Cold War period after 1945 heightened tensions between the world powers. Following Stalin's death in 1953, however, new leadership in the Soviet Union and the United States provided the possibility for discussions to resolve divisive issues affecting Europe. The first major post–World War II summit of national leaders took place in Geneva, Switzerland, in July 1955. Participants included Nikita Khrushchev (Soviet Union), Dwight Eisenhower (United States), Edgar Faure (France), and Anthony Eden (United Kingdom). While no significant breakthroughs occurred, the atmosphere improved in what came to be known as the "Spirit of Geneva." The following "Directive to Foreign Ministers," dated July 23, shows the efforts of the participating states to improve relations.

γ   γ   γ

The Heads of Government of France, the United Kingdom, the U.S.S.R. and the U.S.A., guided by the desire to contribute to the relaxation of international tension and to the consolidation of confidence between states, instruct their Foreign Ministers to continue the consid-

* *Department of State Bulletin*, 33 (August 1, 1955), pp. 176–77.

eration of the following questions with regard to which an exchange of views has taken place at the Geneva Conference, and to propose effective means for their solution, taking account of the close link between the unification of Germany and the problems of European security, and the fact that the successful settlement of each of these problems would serve the interests of consolidating peace.

1. European Security and Germany.
For the purpose of establishing European security with due regard to the legitimate interests of all nations and their inherent right to individual and collective self-defense, the Ministers are instructed to consider various proposals to this end, including the following: A security pact for Europe or for a part of Europe, including provision for the assumption by member nations of an obligation not to resort to force and to deny assistance to an aggressor; limitation, control, and inspection in regard to armed forces and armaments; establishment between East and West of a zone in which the disposition of armed forces will be subject to mutual agreement; and also to consider other possible proposals pertaining to the solution of this problem.

The Heads of Government, recognizing their common responsibility for the settlement of the German question and the re-unification of Germany, have agreed the settlement of the German question and the re-unification of Germany by means of free elections shall be carried out in conformity with the national interests of the German people and the interests of German security. The Foreign Ministers will make whatever arrangements they may consider desirable for the participation of, or for consultation with, other interested parties.

2. Disarmament
The Four Heads of Government,
Desirous of removing the threat of war and lessening the burden of armaments,
Convinced of the necessity, for secure peace and for the welfare of mankind, of achieving a system for the control and reduction of all armaments and armed forces under effective safeguards,
Recognizing that achievements in this field would release vast material resources to be devoted to the peaceful economic development of nations, for raising their well-being, as well as for assistance to underdeveloped countries,

Agree:

(1) for these purposes to work together to develop an acceptable system for disarmament through the Sub-Committee of the United Nations Disarmament Commission;

(2) to instruct their representatives in the Sub-Committee in the discharge of their mandate from the United Nations to take account in their work of the view and proposals advanced by the Heads of Government at this Conference;

(3) to propose that the next meeting of the Sub-Committee to be held on August 29, 1955, at New York;

(4) to instruct the Foreign Ministers to take note of the proceedings in the Disarmament Commission, to take account of the views and proposals advanced by the Heads of Government at this Conference and to consider whether the four Governments can take any further useful initiative in the field of disarmament.

3. Development of Contacts between East and West

The Foreign Ministers should by means of experts study measures, including those possible in organs and agencies of the United Nations, which could (a) bring about a progressive elimination of barriers which interfere with free communications and peaceful trade between people and (b) bring about such freer contacts and exchanges as are to the mutual advantage of the countries and peoples concerned.

4. The Foreign Ministers of the Four Powers will meet at Geneva during October to initiate their consideration of these questions and to determine the organisation of their work.

DOCUMENT NO. 6

THE WARSAW PACT, 1955*

As the East–West Cold War intensified in the post–World War II years after 1945, the United States and the Soviet Union created alliance systems that faced each other in Europe. The Western alliance, the North Atlantic

* U.S. Department of State, *American Foreign Policy, 1950–1955: Basic Documents* (Washington, 1957), I, pp. 1239–42.

Treaty Organization (NATO), was formed in 1949 by the United States and eleven other nations. The Soviet Union established a military alliance with seven East European neighbors in 1955: Albania, Bulgaria, Czechoslovakia, East Germany, Hungary, Poland, and Rumania. Commonly referred to as the "Warsaw Pact," since the formal signing ceremony took place in the Polish capital on May 14, 1955, it also is known as the "Warsaw Security Pact" or the "Warsaw Treaty Organization" (WTO). Despite its Polish title, this alliance of communist states was directed primarily from Moscow which possessed the largest military forces in the WTO and stationed its troops on the territory of its Warsaw Pact allies. This group continued throughout the decades of the Cold War, but with the collapse of communist regimes in Eastern Europe in 1989 and the formation of democratic governments in those states, the unity of the WTO alliance rapidly deteriorated. Finally, under the leadership of Mikhail Gorbachev in the Soviet Union, the WTO was officially terminated in the spring of 1991. NATO, however, continued to exist.

γ   γ   γ

The Contracting Parties, reaffirming their desire for the establishment of a system of European collective security based on the participation of all European states irrespective of their social and political systems, which would make it possible to unite their efforts in safeguarding the peace of Europe; mindful, at the same time, of the situation created in Europe by the ratification of the Paris agreements, which envisage the formation of a new military alignment in the shape of "Western European Union," with the participation of a remilitarized Western Germany and the integration of the latter in the North-Atlantic bloc [NATO], which increased the danger of another war and constitutes a threat to the national security of the peaceable states; being persuaded that in these circumstances the peaceable European states must take the necessary measures to safeguard their security and in the interests of preserving peace in Europe; guided by the objects and principles of the Charter of the United Nations Organization; being desirous of further promoting and developing friendship, cooperation and mutual assistance in accordance with the principles of respect for the independence and sovereignty of states and of non-interference in their internal affairs, have decided to conclude the present Treaty of Friendship, Cooperation and Mutual Assistance and have for that purpose appointed . . .

their plenipotentiaries . . . who, having presented their full powers, found in good and due form, have agreed as follows:

Article 1: The Contracting Parties undertake, in accordance with the Charter of the United Nations Organization, to refrain in their international relations from the threat or use of force, and to settle their international disputes peacefully and in such manner as will not jeopardize international peace and security.

Article 2: The Contracting Parties declare their readiness to participate in a spirit of sincere cooperation in all international actions designed to safeguard international peace and security, and will fully devote their energies to the attainment of this end. The Contracting Parties will furthermore strive for the adoption, in agreement with other states which may desire to cooperate in this, of effective measures for universal reduction of armaments and prohibition of atomic, hydrogen and other weapons of mass destruction.

Article 3: The Contracting Parties shall consult with one another on all important international issues affecting their common interests, guided by the desire to strengthen international peace and security. They shall immediately consult with one another whenever, in the opinion of one of them, a threat of armed attack on one or more of the Parties to the Treaty has arisen, in order to ensure joint defence and the maintenance of peace and security.

Article 4: In the event of armed attack in Europe on one or more of the Parties to the Treaty by any state of group of states, each of the Parties to the Treaty, in the exercise of its right to individual or collective self-defence in accordance with Article 51 of the Charter of the United Nations Organization, shall immediately, either individually or in agreement with other Parties to the Treaty, come to the assistance of the state or states attacked with all such means as it deems necessary, including armed force. The Parties to the Treaty shall immediately consult concerning the necessary measures to be taken by them jointly in order to restore and maintain international peace and security. Measures taken on the basis of this Article shall be reported to the Security Council in conformity with the provisions of the Charter of the United Nations Organization. These measures shall be discontinued immediately

[when] the Security Council adopts the necessary measures to restore and maintain international peace and security.

Article 5: The Contracting Parties have agreed to establish a Joint Command of the armed forces that by agreement among the Parties shall be assigned to the Command, which shall function on the basis of jointly established principles. They shall likewise adopt other agreed measures necessary to strengthen their defensive power, in order to protect the peaceful labours of their peoples, guarantee the inviolability of their frontiers and territories, and provide defence against possible aggression.

Article 6: For the purpose of the consultations among the Parties envisaged in the present Treaty, and also for the purpose of examining questions which may arise in the operation of the Treaty, a Political Consultative Committee shall be set up, in which each of the Parties to the Treaty shall be represented by a member of its Government or by another specifically appointed representative. The Committee may set up such auxiliary bodies as may prove necessary.

Article 7: The Contracting Parties undertake not to participate in any coalitions or alliances and not to conclude any agreements whose objects conflict with the objects of the present Treaty. The Contracting Parties declare that their commitments under existing international treaties do not conflict with the provisions of the present Treaty.

Article 8: The Contracting Parties declare that they will act in a spirit of friendship and cooperation with a view to further developing and fostering economic and cultural intercourse with one another, each adhering to the principle of respect for the independence and sovereignty of the others and non-interference in their internal affairs.

Article 9: The present Treaty is open to the accession of other states, irrespective of their social and political systems, which express their readiness by participation in the present Treaty to assist in uniting the efforts of the peaceable states in safeguarding the peace and security of the peoples. Such accession shall enter into force with the agreement of the Parties to the Treaty after the declaration of accession has been deposited with the Government of the Polish People's Republic.

Article 10: The present Treaty is subject to ratification, and the instruments of ratification shall be deposited with the Government of the Polish People's Republic. The Treaty shall enter into force on the day the last instrument of ratification has been deposited. The Government of the Polish People's Republic shall notify the other Parties to the Treaty as each instrument of ratification is deposited.

Article 11: The present Treaty shall remain in force for twenty years. For such Contracting Parties as do not at least one year before the expiration of this period present to the Government of the Polish People's Republic a statement of denunciation of the Treaty, it shall remain in force for the next ten years. Should a system of collective security be established in Europe, and a General European Treaty of Collective Security concluded for this purpose, for which the Contracting Parties will unswervingly strive, the present Treaty shall cease to be operative from the day the General European Treaty enters into force.

DOCUMENT NO. 7

KHRUSHCHEV'S ANTI-STALIN SPEECH, 1956*

One of the most dramatic events of the post–World War II period was Nikita Khrushchev's speech to the 20th Congress of the Communist Party in which he extensively documented and denounced Joseph Stalin's policies and leadership of the Soviet Union. Given to a closed session of the meeting of high party leaders, the speech was not intended for public knowledge. Copies quickly surfaced, however, and it has been available for all to see in understanding the variety and extent of the "crimes" of the Stalin era.

The speech focused on a number of topics in which, according to Khrushchev, Stalin did not deserve the high reputation as the nation's leader until his death in 1953. Khrushchev detailed the arrests and purges of the 1930s against innocent persons (and confessions extracted by torture); Stalin's inept leadership during World War II; the fabricated "Doctor's Plot" and other contrived conspiracies after the war that led to more arrests and purges

---

* *Congressional Record, 84th Congress, 2nd Session*, CII (June 4, 1956), pp. 9389–9402.

as a way to maintain Stalin's power; and the "cult of personality" that ele-
vated Stalin above Lenin. Khrushchev took a major risk in his denunciation,
for he had been part of Stalin's inner circle since the later 1930s, but he at-
tempted to distance himself from the dictator's policies. The following are ex-
cerpts of this lengthy address given on February 26, 1956, which took ap-
proximately four hours to deliver to the 20th Party delegates.

γ   γ   γ

After Stalin's death the Central Committee of the party began to implement a policy of explaining concisely and consistently that it is im-
permissible and foreign to the spirit of Marxism–Leninism to elevate
one person, to transform him into superman possessing supernatural
characteristics akin to those of a god. Such a man supposedly knows
everything, sees everything, thinks for everyone, can do anything, is infallible in his behavior. Such a belief about a man, and especially about
Stalin, was cultivated among us for many years.

The objective of the present report is not a thorough evaluation of
Stalin's life and activity. . . . At the present we are concerned with a
question which has immense importance for the Party now and for the
future—we are concerned with how the cult of the person of Stalin has
been gradually growing, the cult which became at a certain specified
stage the source of a whole series of exceedingly serious and grave per-
versions of party principles, of party democracy, of revolutionary legality. . . .

During Lenin's life . . . [he] made a completely correct characterization of Stalin, pointing out that it was necessary to consider the question of transferring Stalin from the position of Secretary General because of the fact that Stalin is excessively rude, that he does not have a
proper attitude toward his comrades, that he is capricious, and abuses
his power. . . .

We have to consider seriously and analyze correctly this matter in order
that we may preclude any possibility of a repetition in any form whatever of what took place during the life of Stalin, who absolutely did not
tolerate collegiality in leadership and in work, and who practiced brutal
violence, not only toward everything which opposed him, but also to-

ward that which seemed to his capricious and despotic character, contrary to his concepts.

Stalin acted not through persuasion, explanation, and patient cooperation with people, but by imposing his concepts and demanding absolute submission to his opinion. Whoever opposed this concept or tried to prove his viewpoint, and the correctness of his position, was doomed to removal from the leading collective [party leadership] and to subsequent moral and physical annihilation. This was especially true during the period following the 17th party congress, when many prominent party leaders and rank-and-file party workers, honest and dedicated to the cause of communism, fell victim to Stalin's despotism. . . . This led to glaring violation of revolutionary legality, and to the fact that many entirely innocent persons, who in the past had defended the party line, became victims. . . .

Lenin's wisdom in dealing with people was evident in his work with cadres. An entirely different relationship with people characterized Stalin. . . . He [Stalin] discarded the Leninist method of convincing and educating; he abandoned the method of ideological struggle for that of administrative violence, mass repressions, and terror. He acted on an increasingly larger scale and more stubbornly through punitive organs, at the same time often violating all existing norms of morality and of Soviet laws. . . .

Lenin used severe methods only in the most necessary cases, when the exploiting classes were still in existence and were vigorously opposing the revolution, when the struggle for survival was decidedly assuming the sharpest forms, even including a civil war. Stalin, on the other hand, used extreme methods and mass repressions at a time when the revolution was already victorious, when the Soviet state was strengthened, when the exploiting classes were already liquidated, and socialist relations were rooted solidly in all phases of national economy, when our party was politically consolidated and had strengthened itself both numerically and ideologically. It is clear that here Stalin showed in a whole series of cases his intolerance, his brutality, and his abuse of power. Instead of proving his political correctness and mobilizing the masses, he often chose the path of repression and physical annihilation, not only against actual enemies, but also against individuals who had not committed any crimes against the party and the Soviet government. . . .

In practice Stalin ignored the norms of party life and trampled on the Leninist principle of collective party leadership. . . . It was determined that of the 139 members and candidates of the party's Central Committee who were elected at the 17th congress, 98 persons, that is, 70 percent, were arrested and shot (mostly in 1937–1939). . . . This was the result of the abuse of power by Stalin, who began to use mass terror against the party cadres. . . .

Stalin put the party and the NKVD [the secret police] up to the use of mass terror when the exploiting classes had been liquidated in our country and when there were no serious reasons for the use of extraordinary mass terror. This terror was actually directed not at the remnants of the defeated exploiting classes but against the honest workers of the party and of the Soviet state; against them were made lying, slanderous, and absurd accusations concerning two-facedness, espionage, sabotage, preparation of fictitious plots, and so forth. . . .

Many thousands of honest and innocent Communists have died as a result of this monstrous falsification of such cases, as a result of the fact that all kinds of slanderous confessions were accepted, and as a result of the practice of forcing accusations against oneself and others. In the same manner were fabricated the cases against eminent party and state workers—Kossior, Chubar, Postyshev, Kosaryev, and others. In those years repressions on a mass scale were applied which were based on nothing tangible and which resulted in heavy cadre losses to the party. The vicious practice was condoned of having the NKVD prepare lists of persons whose cases were under the jurisdiction of the military collegium and whose sentences were prepared in advance. Yezhov would send these lists to Stalin personally for his approval of the proposed punishment. In 1937–38, 383 such lists containing the names of many thousands of party, Soviet, Komsomol, army, and economic workers were sent to Stalin. He approved these lists. . . .

Mass arrests of party, Soviet, economic, and military workers caused tremendous harm to our country and to the cause of socialist advancement. Mass repressions had a negative influence on the moral-political condition of the party, created a situation of uncertainty, contributed to the spreading of unhealthy suspicion, and sowed distrust among Communists. All sorts of slanders and careerists were active.

Facts prove that many abuses were made on Stalin's orders without reckoning with any norms of party and Soviet legality. Stalin was a very distrustful man, sickly suspicious; we know this from our work with him. He could look at a man and say: "Why are your eyes so shifty today," or "Why are you turning so much today and avoiding to look me directly in the eyes?" The sickly suspicion created in him a general distrust even toward eminent party workers who he had known for years. Everywhere and in everything he saw enemies, "two-facers" and spies. . . . These and many other facts shows that all norms of correct party solution of problems were invalidated and everything was dependent upon the willfulness of one man.

The power accumulated in the hands of one person, Stalin, led to serious consequences during the great patriotic war [World War II]. When we look at many of our novels, films, and historical scientific studies, the role of Stalin in the patriotic war appears to be entirely improbable. Stalin had foreseen everything. The Soviet Army, on the basis of a strategic plan prepared by Stalin long before, used the tactics of so-called active defense, i.e., tactics which, as we know, allowed the Germans to come up to Moscow and Stalingrad. Using such tactics, the Soviet Army, supposedly thanks only to Stalin's genius, turned to the offensive and subdued the enemy. The epic victory gained through the armed might of the land of the Soviets, through our heroic people, is ascribed in this type of novel, film, and scientific study as being completely due to the strategic genius of Stalin. . . . What are the facts of the matter?. . . .

Documents which have now been published show that by April 3, 1941, Churchill . . . personally warned Stalin that the Germans had begun regrouping their armed units with the intent of attacking the Soviet Union. . . . Churchill stressed this repeatedly in his dispatches of April 18 and in the following days. However, Stalin took no heed of these warnings. What is more, Stalin ordered that no credence be given to information of this sort, in order not to provoke the initiation of military operations. . . .

However, we speak not only about the moment when the war began, which led to serious disorganization of our army and brought us severe losses. Even after the war began, the nervousness and hysteria which Stalin demonstrated, interfering with actual military operations, caused our army serious damage. Stalin was very far from an understanding of the real situation which was developing at the front. . . . Simultaneously, Stalin was interfering with operations and issuing orders which did not take into consideration the real situation at a given section of the front and which could not help but result in huge personnel losses. . . . And what was the result of this? The worst that we had expected. The Germans surrounded our army concentrations and consequently we lost hundreds of thousands of our soldiers. This is Stalin's military genius; this is what it cost us. . . .

We must state that after the war the situation became even more complicated. Stalin became even more capricious, irritable, and brutal. In particular his suspicion grew. His persecution mania reached unbelievable dimensions. Many workers were becoming enemies before his very eyes. After the war Stalin separated himself from the collective [party leadership] even more. Everything was decided by him alone without any consideration for anyone or anything. . . . You see to what Stalin's mania for greatness led. He had completely lost consciousness of reality; he demonstrated his suspicion and haughtiness not only in relation to individuals in the U.S.S.R. but in relation to whole parties and nations. . . .

Comrades, the cult of the individual acquired such monstrous size, chiefly because Stalin himself, using all conceivable methods, supported the glorification of his own person. This is supported by numerous facts. One of the most characteristic examples of Stalin's self-glorification and of his lack of even elementary modesty is the edition of his Short Biography, which was published in 1948. This book is an expression of the most dissolute flattery, an example of making a man into a godhead, of transforming him into an infallible sage, "the greatest leader," "sublime strategist of all times and nations." Finally, no other words would be found with which to lift Stalin up to the heavens. We need not give here examples of the loathsome adulation filling this book. All we need to add is that they all were approved and edited by Stalin personally and some of them were added in his own handwriting to the draft text of the book. . . . In speaking about the events of the [1917] October Revolution and about the civil war [1918–1920], the impression was created that Stalin always played the main role, as if everywhere and always Stalin had suggested to Lenin what to do and how to do it. However, this is slander of Lenin. . . .

Comrades, the cult of the individual has caused the employment of faulty principles in party work and in economic activity. It brought about rule violation of internal party and Soviet democracy, sterile administration, deviations of all sorts, covering up of shortcomings and varnishing of reality. . . . We should also not forget that due to the numerous arrests of party, Soviet and economic leaders, many workers began to work uncertainly, showed overcautiousness, feared all which was new, feared their own shadows and began to show less initiative in their work. . . .

Stalin separated himself from the people and never went anywhere. This lasted tens of years. The last time he visited a village was in January 1928 when he visited Siberia in connection with grain deliveries. How then could he have known the situation in the provinces? . . . If Stalin said anything, it meant it was so—after all, he was a genius and a genius does not need to count, he only needs to look and can immediately tell how it should be. When he expresses his opinion, everyone has to repeat it and to admire his vision. . . . Stalin often failed for months to take up some unusually important problems concerning the life of the party and of the state whose solution could not be postponed. During Stalin's leadership our peaceful relations with other nations were often threatened, because one-man decisions could cause and often did cause great complications. . . .

Comrades, in order not to repeat errors of the past, the central committee has declared itself resolutely against this cult of the individual. We consider that Stalin was excessively extolled. However, in the past Stalin doubtlessly performed great services to the party, to the working class, and to the international workers' movement. This question is complicated by the fact that all this which we have just discussed was done during Stalin's life under his leadership and with his concurrence; here Stalin was convinced that this was necessary for the defense of the interests of the working classes against the plotting of the enemies and against the attacks of the imperialist camp. He saw this from the position of the interest of the working class, of the interest of the laboring people, of the interest of the victory of socialism and communism. We cannot say that these were the deeds of a giddy despot. He considered that this should be done in the interests of the party, of the working masses, in the name of the defense of the revolution's gains. In this lies the whole tragedy. . . .

We should in all seriousness consider the question of the cult of the individual. We cannot let this matter get out of the party, especially not to the press. It is for this reason that we are considering it here at a closed congress session. We should know the limits; we should not give ammunition to the enemy; we should not wash our dirty linen before their eyes. I think that the delegates to the congress will understand and assess properly all these proposals. . . .

DOCUMENT NO. 8

BRITISH POLICY IN THE SUEZ CRISIS, 1956*

The post–World War II era saw the rise of nationalistic and independence movements in numerous European colonies in Asia and Africa, and the resistance to European domination succeeded in many regions in the 1950s and 1960s. Egypt, with its vital Suez Canal, had been under British control for decades. In the mid-1950s, a charismatic Egyptian leader came to power who became a rallying point not only for his country but also for other nationalistic movements in the Middle East. Gamal Abdul Nasser illustrated the decline of European colonial empires. He also established relations with the Soviet Union and communist regimes in Eastern Europe which made Nasser even more suspect in the eyes of Western governments. Although

* From *Full Circle: The Memoirs of Anthony Eden*. Copyright (c) 1960 by Times Publishing Company Ltd. Reprinted by permission of Houghton Mifflin Company. All Rights Reserved.

Egypt possessed no oil resources, the Suez Canal provided a vital shipping link connecting Europe and Asia. Nasser demanded its return to Egyptian control, and when negotiations failed to resolve the issue, his government declared the canal was now under total Egyptian authority. The following is a September 5, 1956 letter from British Prime Minister Anthony Eden to U.S. President Dwight Eisenhower, outlining British concerns about Nasser's actions and Eden's proposed response to the crisis. In addition to the canal issue as the immediate problem, he referred to the need for Middle Eastern oil to meet European and Western energy requirements. He also interpreted the lack of any Western action against Nasser as repeating Europe's appeasement of Adolf Hitler in the 1930s. British French, and Israeli military forces attacked Egypt in October 1956.

γ   γ   γ

Thank you for your message and writing thus frankly. There is no doubt as to where we are agreed and have been agreed from the very beginning, namely that we should do everything we can to get a peaceful settlement. It is in this spirit that we favoured calling the twenty-two-power conference and that we have worked in the closest co-operation with you about this business since. There has never been any question of our suddenly or without further provocation resorting to arms, while these processes were at work. In any event, as your own wide knowledge would confirm, we could not have done this without extensive preparation lasting several weeks.

This question of precautions has troubled me considerably and still does. I have not forgotten the riots and murders in Cairo in 1952, for I was in charge here at the time when Winston [Winston Churchill, at that time the British Prime Minister] was on the high seas on his way back from the United States.

We are both agreed that we must give the Suez committee every chance to fulfill their mission. This is our firm resolve. If the committee and subsequent negotiations succeed in getting Nasser's agreement to the London proposals of the eighteen powers, there will be no call for force. But if the committee fails, we must have some immediate alternative which will show that Nasser is not going to get his way. In this connection we are attracted by Foster's [U.S. Secretary of State John Foster Dulles] suggestion, if I understand it rightly, for the running of the canal by the users in virtue of their rights under the 1888 Convention. We heard about this from our Embassy in Washington yesterday. I think that we could go along with this, provided that the intention was made clear by both of us immediately the Menzies mission finishes its work. But unless we can proceed with this, or something very like it, what should the next step be?

You suggest that this is where we diverge. If that is so I think that the divergence springs from a difference in our assessment of Nasser's plans and intentions. May I set out our view of the position.

In the nineteen-thirties Hitler established his position by a series of carefully planned movements. These began with occupation of the Rhineland and were followed by successive acts of aggression against Austria, Czechoslovakia, Poland and the West. His actions were tolerated and excused by the majority of the population of Western Europe. It was argued either that Hitler had committed no act of aggression against anyone, or that he was entitled to do what he liked in his own territory, or that it was impossible to prove that he had any ulterior designs, or that the Covenant of the League of Nations did not entitle us to use force and that it would be wiser to wait until he did commit an act of aggression.

In more recent years Russia has attempted similar tactics. The blockade of Berlin was to have been the opening move in a campaign designed at least to deprive the Western powers of their whole position in Germany. On this occasion we fortunately reacted at once with the result that the Russian design was never unfolded. But I am sure that you would agree that it would be wrong to infer from this circumstance that no Russian design existed.

Similarly the seizure of the Suez Canal is, we are convinced, the opening gambit in a planned campaign designed by Nasser to expel all Western influence and interests from Arab countries. He believes that if he can get away with this, and if he can successfully defy eighteen nations, his prestige in Arabia will be so great that he will be able to mount revolutions of young officers in Saudi Arabia, Jordan, Syria and Iraq. (We know that he is already preparing a revolution in Iraq, which is most stable and progressive.) These new Governments will in effect be Egyptian satellites if not Russian ones. They will have to place their united oil resources under the control of a united Arabia led by Egypt and under Russian influence. When that moment comes Nasser can deny oil to Western Europe and we here shall be at his mercy.

There are some who doubt whether Saudi Arabia, Iraq and Kuwait will be prepared even for a time to sacrifice their oil revenues for the sake of Nasser's ambitions. But if we place ourselves in their position I think the dangers are clear. If Nasser says to them, "I have nationalized the Suez Canal. I have successfully defied eighteen powerful nations including the United States, I have defied the whole of the United Nations in the matter of the Israel blockade, I have expropriated all Western property. Trust me and withhold oil from Western Europe. Within six months or a year, the continent of Europe will be on its knees before you," will the Arabs not be prepared to follow his lead? Can we rely on them to be more sensible than were the Germans? Even if the Arabs eventually fall apart again as they did after the early Caliphs, the damage will have been done meanwhile.

In short we are convinced that if Nasser is allowed to defy the eighteen nations it will be a matter of months before revolution breaks out in the oil-bearing countries and the West is wholly deprived of Middle Eastern oil. In this belief we are fortified by the advice of friendly leaders in the Middle East. The Iraqis are the most insistent in their warnings; both Nuri and the Crown Prince have spoken to us several times of the consequences of Nasser succeeding in his grab. They would be swept away. . . .

The difference which separates us to-day appears to be a difference of assessment of Nasser's plans and intentions and of the consequences in the Middle East of military action against him. You may feel that even if we are right it would be better to wait until Nasser has unmistakably unveiled his intentions. But this was the argument which prevailed in 1936 and which we both rejected in 1948. Admittedly there are risks in the use of force against Egypt now. It is, however, clear that military intervention designed to reverse Nasser's revolutions in the whole continent would be a much more costly and difficult undertaking. I am very troubled, as it is, that if we do not reach a conclusion either way about the canal very soon one or other of these Eastern lands may be toppled at any moment by Nasser's revolutionary movements.

I agree with you that prolonged military operations as well as the denial of Middle East oil would place an immense strain on the economy of Western Europe. I can assure you that we are conscious of the burdens and perils attending military intervention. But if our assessment is correct, and if the only alternative is to allow Nasser's plans quietly to develop until this country and all Western Europe are held to ransom by Egypt acting at Russia's behest it seems to us that our duty is plain. We have many times led Europe in the fight for freedom. It would be an ignoble end of our long history if we accepted to perish by degree.

DOCUMENT NO. 9

U.S. POLICY DURING THE SUEZ CRISIS, 1956*

The Middle East faced numerous confrontations, crises, and conflicts in the 1950s. Antagonism between Israel and Egypt, already tense, reached new heights in 1955–56. The actions of Egypt, a former British colony, also created serious problems with Great Britain and France in the summer and fall of 1956. This included the takeover of the Suez Canal and also the largely British-and French-owned Suez Canal Company. As the situation deteriorated, Israel, Britain and France held secret talks to plan joint military operations against Egypt. This led to Israeli forces invading Egyptian territory in late October, immediately followed by similar military action by the British and French. The United Nations attempted to stop the conflict by calling for a cease-fire by all combatants. The following are excerpts of comments of the American Secretary of State, John Foster Dulles, made to an emergency meeting of the United Nations General Assembly on November 1st, in which he supported a cease-fire in the region and also expressed sadness that the United States had to criticize the governments and actions of three of its friends and allies.

γ   γ   γ

I doubt that any delegate ever spoke from this forum with as heavy a heart as I have brought here tonight. We speak on a matter of vital importance, where the United States finds itself unable to agree with three

* *Department of State Bulletin*, 35 (November 11, 1956), pp. 751–55.

nations with whom it has ties, deep friendship, admiration, and respect, and two of whom constitute our oldest, most trusted and reliable allies.

The fact that we differ with such friends has led us to reconsider and reevaluate our position with the utmost care, and that has been done at the highest levels of our Government. Even after that reevaluation, we still find ourselves in disagreement. Because it seems to us that that disagreement involves principles which far transcend the immediate issue, we feel impelled to make our point of view known to you and through you to the world. . . .

What are the facts that bring us here? There is, first of all, the fact that there occurred beginning last Monday a deep penetration of Egypt by Israeli forces. Then, quickly following upon this action, there came action by France and the United Kingdom in subjecting Egypt first to a 12-hour ultimatum and then to armed attack, which is now going on from the air with the declared purpose of gaining temporary control of the Suez Canal, presumably to make it more secure.

Then there is the third fact that the matter, having been brought to the [United Nations] Security Council, was sought to be dealt with by a resolution which was vetoed by the United Kingdom and by France, which cast the only dissenting votes against the resolution.

Thereupon . . . the matter came here under a call from the [United Nations] Secretary-General, instituted by a vote of seven members of the Security Council, requiring that this [General] Assembly convene in emergency session within 24 hours.

Now, Mr. President and fellow delegates, the United States recognizes full well that the facts which I have referred to are not the only facts in this situation. There is a long and sad history of irritations and of provocations. There have been armistice violations by Israel and against Israel. There have been violations by Egypt of the treaty of 1888 governing the Suez Canal, and a disregard by Egypt of the Security Council resolution of 1951 calling for the passage through that canal of Israeli ships and cargoes. There has been a heavy rearmament of Egypt under somewhat ominous circumstances. There was the abrupt seizure by Egypt of the Universal Suez Canal Company, which largely under British and French auspices had been operating that canal ever since it was opened 90 years ago. There have been repeated expressions of hostility by the Government of Egypt toward other governments with whom it ostensibly had, and should have, friendly relations.

We are not blind, Mr. President, to the fact that what has happened in the last 2 or 3 days comes out of a murky background. But we have come to the conclusion that these provocations, serious as they are, cannot justify the resort to armed force which has occurred with the last 2 and 3 days and which is going on tonight.

To be sure, the United Nations perhaps has not done all that it should have done. . . . The United Nations may have been somewhat laggard, somewhat impotent in dealing with many injustices which are inherent in this Middle Eastern situation. But I think that we ought, and I hope will . . . give our most earnest thought to the problem of how we can do more to establish and to implement principles of justice and of international law. We have not done all that we should have done in that respect, and on that account part of the responsibility of present events lies here at our doorstep.

But . . . if we were to agree that the existence of injustices in the world, which this organization so far has been unable to cure, means that the principle of renunciation of force is no longer respected and that there still exists the right wherever a nation feels itself subject to injustice to resort to force to try to correct that injustice, then . . . we would have, I fear, torn this charter into shreds and the world would again be a world of anarchy. And all the great hopes that are placed in this organization and in our charter would have vanished, and we would be, as we were when World War II began, with only another tragic failure in place of what we hoped would be—and still can hope will be—a barrier against the recurrence of a world war which, as our preamble says, has "twice in our lifetime . . . brought untold sorrow to mankind."

Now . . . this problem of the Suez Canal, which lies at the base perhaps in considerable part of the forcible action now being taken, had been dealt with over the past 3 months in many ways and on many occasions. I doubt if in all history so sincere, so sustained an effort has been made to find a just and a peaceful solution.

When on July 26 the Universal Suez Canal Company was abruptly seized by the Egyptian Government, all the world felt that a crisis of momentous proportions had been precipitated. Within, I think, 3 days after the event, the Governments of the United States, the United Kingdom, and France met together in London to see what to do about the situation. Already at that time there were voices raised in favor of an immediate resort to force to attempt to restore the status quo ante the Egyptian seizure. But it was the judgment of all three of our Governments that that resort to force would be unjustified, certainly under the then conditions, and that first efforts should be made to bring about a peaceful and just solution.

Instead of any resort to force at that critical moment, the three Governments agreed to call a conference of the principal users of the Suez Canal—24 nations representing the clearly surviving signatories of the convention of 1888, eight countries who principally used the canal, and eight countries whose pattern of traffic showed particular dependence upon the canal. And 22 of those 24 nations met. Egypt declined. Of the 22, 18 agreed upon what they thought were sound principles for arriving at a peaceful solution, which would be just and fair and which would secure for the future the open use of this waterway. That agreement of the 18 was carried as a proposal to Cairo and presented to President [Gamal] Nasser, who rejected it.

Then the 18 met again in London and again considered a proposal to create an association, a cooperative group of the users. We felt that that association might be able to work out on a practical provisional basis with the Egyptian canal authorities an acceptable arrangement for assuring the operation on a free and impartial basis of the canal. Then while that was in process of being organized—the Users Association—the matter was brought to the Security Council of the United Nations by France and the United Kingdom. There six principles were unanimously adopted with the concurrence of Egypt, who participated in the proceedings though not a member of the council. Those principles were in essence the same principles that had been adopted by the 18 nations in London. There was a second part of the resolution which looked forward to the implementation of these principles. That part failed of adoption, this time by a veto of the Soviet Union. . . .

I recall that at the close of our session of the Security Council, I made a statement which was concurred in, or acquiesced in, by all present, stating that the Security Council remains seized of the problem and that it was hoped that the exchange of views with the Secretary-General and the three countries most directly concerned—Egypt, France, and the United Kingdom—that those discussions and exchanges of views would continue.

They did not continue, although I am not aware of an insuperable obstacle to such a continuance. Instead there developed the events which I have referred to, the invocation of violence, first by Israel and then by France and the United Kingdom, the events which again brought the matter to the Security Council and which, in the face of veto, has brought the matter here to us tonight.

Surely I think we must feel that the peaceful processes which the charter requests every member to follow had not been exhausted. Even in the case of Israel, which has a legitimate complaint due to the fact that Egypt has never complied with the 1951 resolution of the Security Council recognizing Israel's right to use of the canal—even there, there was a better prospect because the principles adopted by the Security Council, with the concurrence of Egypt, called for the passage of ships and cargoes through the canal without discrimination and provided that the canal could not be used or abused for the national purposes of any nation, including Egypt.

So . . . there seemed to be peaceful processes that were at work and which, as I say, had not yet, it seemed to us at least, run their course. And while . . . I would be the last to say that there can never be circumstances where resort to force may not be employed . . . it seems to us that, under the circumstances which I described, the resort to force, the violent armed attack by three of our members upon a fourth, cannot be treated as other than a grave error, inconsistent with the principles and purposes of the charter and one which if persisted in would gravely undermine our charter and undermine this organization. . . .

The question then is: What do we do? . . . . Now, I recognize full well that a recommendation which merely is directed to a cease-fire, to getting back of the armistice lines the foreign land forces in Egypt which so far as we are aware today are only those of Israel, of stopping the attacks by air and not bringing new belligerent forces into the area, and then, as rapidly as possible of the reopening of the Suez Canal—that a resolution which puts primary emphasis upon these things is not an adequate or comprehensive treatment of the situation. All of us, I think, would hope that out of this tragedy there should come something better than merely a restoration of the conditions out of which this tragedy came about. There must be something better than that. Surely this organization has a duty to strive to bring about that betterment. If we should do only that, we too would be negligent and would have dealt only with one aspect of the problem. . . .

I do not by the form of this resolution want to seem in any way to believe that this situation can be adequately taken care of merely by the steps that are in this resolution. There needs to be something better than the uneasy armistices which have existed now for these 8 years between Israel and the Arab neighbors. There needs to be a greater sense of confidence and security in the free and equal operation of the canal than has existed since 3 months ago when President Nasser seized the Suez Canal Company. These things I regard of the utmost importance.

But . . . if we say that it is all right for the fighting to go on until these difficult and complicated matters have been settled, then I fear a situation will have been created such that no settlement will be possible, that the war will have intensified and may have spread, that the world will have been divided by new bitternesses, and that the foundations for peace will have been tragically shattered. . . .

But I think we must put first things first. I believe that the first thing is to stop the fighting as rapidly as possible lest it become a conflagration which would endanger us all—and that is not beyond the realm of possibility. As President Eisenhower said last night, the important thing is to limit and extinguish the fighting insofar as it is possible and as promptly as possible.

I hope . . . that this point of view reflected in this resolution will prevail. I fear that if we do not act and act promptly, and if we do not act with sufficient unanimity of opinion so that our recommendations carry a real influence, there is great danger that what is started and what has been called a police action may develop into something which is far more grave. Even if that does not happen, the apparent impotence of this organization to deal with this situation may set a precedent which will lead other nations to attempt to take into their own hands the remedying of what they believe to be their injustices. If that happens, the future is dark indeed.

We thought when we wrote the [United Nations] charter in San Francisco in 1945 that we had seen perhaps the worst in war, that our task was to prevent a recurrence of what had been, and indeed what then had been was tragic enough. But now we know that what can be will be infinitely more tragic than what we saw in World War II. I believe that at this critical juncture we owe the highest duty to ourselves, to our peoples, to posterity, to take action which will assure that this fire which has started shall not spread but shall promptly be extinguished. Then we shall turn with renewed vigor to curing the injustices out of which this trouble has arisen.

DOCUMENT NO. 10

SOVIET POLICY IN HUNGARY, 1956*

Events in Hungary in 1956 revealed the growing weakening of communism in East Europe. Calls for political, economic, and social reform in Hungary (and Poland) grew during the summer and fall among students and workers. A new government of moderate communist leaders replaced the old and unpopular regime in Budapest, and conditions looked positive for a more democratic future for the Hungarian people. Moscow, however, was unwilling to see the decline of its influence in East Europe and military forces intervened in November to repress the reform movement of the new government and revised party leadership. They soon regained control of Budapest and the country, resulting in high numbers of casualties among those resisting the in-

* http://cwihp.si.edu.

vasion. The following is a report of the Soviet Union's Minister of Defense
Georgi Zhukov to Nikita Khrushchev and top Soviet leaders, summarizing
the operations while in progress. Imre Nagy, the new reform Prime Minis-
ter, was arrested and executed along with other Hungarian leaders. Minor
changes have been made in this translation of the document that appeared in
the Cold War International History Project Bulletin.

γ   γ   γ

Report on the situation in Hungary as of 12 noon, 4 November 1956:

At 6:15 on Nov 4, Soviet troops began to conduct the operation for restoring order and rehabilitating the government of the People's Democracy of Hungary. Acting according to an earlier thought-out plan, our
units mastered the most stubborn points of the reaction in the provinces, as they existed in Dier, Miskolc, Debrecen, and even in other regional centers in Hungary. In the course of the operation Soviet troops
occupied the most important communication centers, including the
power radio broadcasting station in Soinok, the depots of military supplies and weapons, and other important military objectives.

The Soviet troops operating in Budapest, having broken the resistance
of the insurgents, occupied the Parliament building, the Central Committee of the Hungarian Workers Party, and even the radio station in
the region near the Parliament building. Also seized were three bridges
across the Dunai [Danube] River, joining the eastern and western parts
of the city, and the arsenal of weapons and military supplies.

The whole staff of the counterrevolutionary government of Imre Nagy
was in hiding. Searches are being conducted. One large hotbed of resistance of the insurgents remains in Budapest around the Corwin Thea-
ter in the southern-eastern part of the city. The insurgents defending
this stubborn point were presented with an ultimatum to capitulate. In
connection with the refusal of the resisters to surrender, the troops began an assault on them.

The main garrisons of the Hungarian troops were blockaded. Many of
them gave up their weapons without a serious fight. Instructions were
given to our troops to return the captured insurgents to the command

of Hungarian officers and to arrest the officers who were assigned to replace the captured ones.

With the objective of not allowing the penetration of Hungary by the hostile agency and the escape of the resistance leaders from Hungary, our troops have occupied the Hungarian airports and solidly closed off all the roads on the Austro-Hungarian border. The troops, continuing to fulfill the assignment, are purging the territory of Hungary of insurgents.

DOCUMENT NO. 11

IMRE NAGY'S FINAL MESSAGE, 1956*

The Soviet Union's military intervention in Hungary in November 1956 crushed the reform movement that had emerged that year. Imre Nagy, a moderate Communist, became the nation's new Prime Minister on October 24th and many looked to him to lead Hungary toward a more democratic and successful future. As fighting raged in the streets of the capital city of Budapest, Nagy broadcast the following announcement on November 4, 1956. He took refuge in the Yugoslav embassy in Budapest, but eventually left the building on promises of his personal safety. However, Soviet authorities immediately arrested Nagy and he was executed. Many years later, following the collapse of the Communist regime in Hungary in 1989, his remains were given an official state funeral at which thousands of Hungarians paid tribute to their fallen leader.

γ   γ   γ

This is Imre Nagy speaking, the President of the Council of Ministers of the Hungarian People's Republic. Today at daybreak Soviet troops attacked our capital with the obvious intention of overthrowing the legal Hungarian democratic Government. Our troops are in combat. The Government is at its post. I notify the people of our country and the entire world of this fact. This fight is the fight for freedom by the Hun-

---

* By permission of United Nations General Assembly, *Report of the Special Committee on the Problem of Hungary* (New York, 1957), pp. 45–46.

garian people against the Russian intervention, and it is possible that I shall only be able to stay at my post for one or two hours. The whole world will see how the Russian armed forces, contrary to all treaties and conventions, are crushing the resistance of the Hungarian people. They will also see how they are kidnapping the Prime Minister of a country which is a Member of the United Nations, taking him from the capital, and therefore it cannot be doubted at all that this is the most brutal form of intervention. I should like in these last moments to ask the leaders of the revolution, if they can, to leave the country. I ask that all that I have said in my broadcast, and what we have agreed on with the revolutionary leaders during meetings in Parliament, should be put in a memorandum, and the leaders should turn to all the people of the world for help and explain that today it is Hungary and tomorrow, or the day after tomorrow, it will be the turn of other countries, because the imperialism of Moscow does not know borders and is only trying to play for time.

DOCUMENT NO. 12

THE COMMON MARKET, 1957*

The devastating effects of World War II weakened the economies and political systems in postwar Europe. This played a significant role in convincing several governments of the need to work cooperatively to achieve mutual economic benefit. Negotiations led to the formation in 1951 of the European Coal and Steel Community (Document 2) in 1951 to more closely link the industrial economies of six nations: Belgium, France, Italy, Luxembourg, Netherlands, and West Germany. The success of the ECSC convinced these governments to expand their cooperation in which most or all commodities could cross their borders without tariffs or other economic impediments. Negotiations culminated in the Treaty of Rome, signed March 25, 1957, to establish the European Community (soon designated as the European Economic Community or EEC), an association that became widely known as the "Common Market." Its success resulted in other nations joining the association, reaching a total of fifteen member states by 1995. The following is a portion of the Treaty of Rome.

* http://europa.eu.int/abc/obj/treaties/en/entr6b.htm#12.

γ   γ   γ

[The governments of Belgium, France, Italy, Luxembourg, Netherlands, and West Germany]

Determined to lay the foundation of an ever closer union among the peoples of Europe,

Resolved to ensure the economic and social progress of their countries by common action to eliminate the barriers which divide Europe,

Affirming as the essential objective of their efforts the constant improvements of the living and working conditions of their people,

Recognizing that the removal of existing obstacles calls for concerted action in order to guarantee steady expansion, balanced trade and fair competition,

Anxious to strengthen the unity of their economies and to ensure their harmonious development by reducing the differences existing between the various regions and the backwardness of the less favoured regions,

Desiring to contribute, by means of a common commercial policy, to the progressive abolition of restrictions on international trade,

Intending to confirm the solidarity which binds Europe and the overseas countries and desiring to ensure the development of their prosperity, in accordance with the principles of the Charter of the United Nations,

Resolved by thus pooling their resources to preserve and strengthen peace and liberty, and calling upon the other peoples of Europe who share their ideas to join in their efforts,

Have decided to create a European Community. . . .

Article 1: By this Treaty, the High Contracting Parties establish among themselves a European Community.

Article 2: The Community shall have as its task, by establishing a common market and an economic and monetary union and by implementing the common policies or activities referred to in Articles 3 and 3a, to promote through the Community a harmonious and balanced development of economic activities, sustained and non-inflationary growth respecting the environment, a high degree of convergence of economic performance, a high level of employment and of social protection, the raising the the standard of living and quality of life, and economic and social cohesion and solidarity among Member States.

Article 3: For the purposes set out in Article 2, the activities of the

Community shall include, as provided in this Treaty and in accordance with the timetable set out therein:

a. the elimination, as between Member States, of customs duties and quantitative restrictions on the import and export of goods, and of all other measures having equivalent effect;

b. a common commercial policy;

c. an internal market characterized by the abolition, as between Member States, of obstacles to the free movement of goods, persons, services and capital;

d. measures concerning the entry and movement of persons in the internal market . . . ;

e. a common policy in the sphere of agriculture and fisheries;

f. a common policy in the sphere of transport;

g. a system ensuring that competition in the internal market is not distorted;

h. the approximation of the laws of Member States to the extent required for the functioning of the common market;

i. a policy in the social sphere comprising a European Social Fund;

j. the strengthening of economic and social cohesion;

k. a policy in the sphere of the environment;

l. the strengthening of the competitiveness of Community industry;

m. the promotion of research and technological development;

n. encouragement for the establishment and development of trans European networks;

o. a contribution to the attainment of a high level of health protection;

p. a contribution to education and training of quality and to the flowering of the cultures of the Member States;

q. a policy in the sphere of development cooperation;

r. the association of the overseas countries and territories in order to increase trade and promote jointly economic and social development;

s. a contribution to the strengthening of consumer protection;

t. measures in the spheres of energy, civil protection and tourism.

Article 3a:

1. For the purposes set out in Article 2, the activities of the Member States and the Community shall include, as provided in this Treaty and in accordance with the timetable set out therein, the adoption of an economic policy which is based on the close coordination of Member States' economic policies, on the internal market and on the definition

of common objectives, and conducted in accordance with the principle of an open market economy with free competition.

2. Concurrently with the foregoing and as provided in this Treaty and in accordance with the timetable and the procedures set out therein, these activities shall included the irrevocable fixing of exchange rates leading to the introduction of a single currency, the ECU, and the definition and conduct of a single monetary policy and exchange rate policy the primary objective of which shall be to maintain price stability and, without prejudice to this objective, to support the general economic policies in the Community, in accordance with the principle of an open market economy with free competition. . . .

DOCUMENT NO. 13

BORIS PASTERNAK AND THE ZHIVAGO CONTROVERSY, 1956–1958*

Russian novelist Boris Pasternak wrote Dr. Zhivago, a novel set in Russia in the early 20th century during the period of war and revolution, and attempted to publish it in the Soviet Union. The official response declared his work as unworthy of publication, accusing him of presenting anti-communist views through the lives and statements of his fictional characters. The book appeared in the West in 1958 to very positive reviews, and the Nobel Committee awarded him the Nobel Prize for Literature for that year. Pasternak was not permitted to attend the ceremony in Stockholm, however, and he faced continued harassment in the Soviet Union for this work that gained such world renown. In 1958 he was expelled from the Union of Soviet Writers, and until his death in 1960, never permitted to publish any further literary works in his country. Only in the 1990s, after the collapse of the Soviet Union, was the book published in full in Russia. The following are excerpts of a lengthy 1956 assessment of the book by the editors of "Novy Mir," a leading Soviet literary journal, published in "Literaturnaya Gazeta" in October 1958 to reach a wider audience. It criticized Pasternak for what they said were ideological and historical failings, and this negative assessment

---

* Translation copyright (1958) by *The Current Digest of the Soviet Press*, published weekly at Columbus, Ohio. Reprinted by permission of the *Digest*.

was used to justify the government's refusal to allow Pasternak to attend the Nobel ceremony and accept the literary prize.

γ   γ   γ

Boris Leonidovich [Pasternak],

We, the writers of this letter, have read the manuscript of your novel "Doctor Zhivago," submitted by you to Novy Mir, and want to express openly to you all our thoughts that grew out of this reading. They are alarming and grave thoughts.

We realize that if it were simply a matter of "likes or dislikes," a matter of taste or even of radical but purely artistic differences, you might not be interested in such esthetic squabbles. "Yes, yes!" or "No, no!" you might say. "The magazine has rejected the manuscript; so much the worse for the magazine, but the artist continues to believe in its esthetic worth."

However, in this instance the question is a more complex one. The thing that alarmed us in your novel is something that neither the editors nor the author could change by partial deletions or corrections. We are concerned here with the very spirit of the novel, with its pathos and with the author's view of life as that view really is or, in any case, as it is formed in the mind of the reader. We feel it is our direct duty to speak to you about this as people to whose views you may or may not attach importance, but whose collective opinion you have no grounds for considering prejudiced and which, therefore, is at least worth hearing out.

The spirit of your novel is the sprit of nonacceptance of the socialist revolution. The pathos of your novel is the pathos of the assertion that the October Revolution [1917] and Civil War [1918–1920] and the social changes that followed them brought the people nothing but suffering and destroyed the Russian intelligentsia either physically or morally. The author's views on our country's past and, above all, on the first decade after the October Revolution . . . boil down to the statement that the October Revolution was a mistake, that participation in it by that segment of the intelligentsia that supported it was an irreparable disaster, and that everything that followed from it was evil. . . .

The novel gives no real picture of the country or the people, nor does it show why the revolution in Russia became inevitable or the intolerable degree of suffering and social injustice that brought the people to this revolution. . . . The characters in the novel, and above all Doctor Zhivago himself and his family, spend the years of the revolution and the Civil War in search of relative well-being—a full belly and tranquility amid all the vicissitudes of struggle and at a time of general national ruin. Physically, they are not cowards . . . but at the same time their sole aim is to save their own lives, and it is to this end above all that all their major actions are directed. . . . It is our view that Doctor Zhivago is, in fact, the incarnation of a definite type of Russian intellectual of that day, a man fond of talking about the sufferings of the people and able to discuss them, but unable to cure those sufferings in either the literal or the figurative sense of the word. He is the type of man consumed with a sense of his own singularity, his intrinsic value, a man far removed from the people and ready to betray them in difficult times, to cut himself off from their sufferings and their cause. . . .

Such is the philosophy of your novel's chief protagonist, a man who could no more be removed from it than a soul could be removed from a body. Such is the progression of his thoughts about the revolution; such is his prosecutor's tone; such is the strength of his hatred for the revolution. . . .

Doctor Zhivago has ambivalent feelings: There is enough hatred of the revolution in him for two Denikens [a general who fought against the communists in the Russian Civil War], but because at the same time he considers his own ego to be the most valuable thing in the world, he is unwilling to risk the safety of this ego by committing any outright counter-revolutionary action and while long since committed to that side in spirit, he continues to stand between the two camps in body. . . .

The content of his individualism is the self-glorification of his own psychic essence, raised to a point of equating it with some sort of prophetic mission. Zhivago is not merely a doctor, he is a poet. And to convince the reader that his poetry has true significance for mankind, which is how he understands it himself, you end your novel with a collection of your hero's poetry. In doing so you sacrifice the better part of your own poetic talent to this character you have created in order to exalt hm in the reader's eyes and, at the same time, to identify him as closely with yourself as possible. . . . Thus under cover of an outward sensitivity and morality there arises the figure of a man who is essentially immoral, who acknowledges no responsibility to the people, claiming only rights, including the right—allegedly permitted to supermen—of betrayal with impunity. . . .

You are no stranger to symbolism, and the death, or rather the passing, of Doctor Zhivago in the late 1920s is for you, we feel, a symbol of the death of the Russian intelligentsia, destroyed by the revolution. Yes, it must be admitted that for the Doctor Zhivago you depicted in the novel the climate of the revolution is deadly. And our disagreement with you is not over this but, as we have already mentioned, over something quite different.

To you, Doctor Zhivago is the peak of the spirit of the Russian intelligentsia. To us, he is its swamp. To you, the members of the Russian intelligentsia who took a different path from the one Doctor Zhivago took and who chose the course of serving the people betrayed their true calling, committed spiritual suicide and created nothing of value. To us they found their true calling on precisely that path and continued to serve the people and to do for the people precisely the things that had been done for them—in laying the groundwork for the revolution—by the best segment of the Russian intelligentsia, which was then, and is today, infinitely remote from that conscious break with the people and ideological renegacy [sic] of which your Doctor Zhivago is the bearer.

To all that we have said there remains for us to add, with bitter regret, only a few words about how the people are depicted in your novel during the years of the revolution. This depiction, given mainly through Doctor Zhivago's eyes but at times in the form of direct narrative, is extremely characteristic of the anti-popular spirit of your novel and profoundly contradicts the whole tradition of Russian literature which, while never fawning over the people, was, nonetheless, capable of seeing their beauty, their strength and their spiritual richness. But the people as depicted in your novel are divided into the good-hearted wanderers who cling to Doctor Zhivago and those close to him, and the creatures, half man, half beast, who personify the elemental forces of the revolution—or rather, as you see it, of the insurrection, the riot. . . .

As yet we have hardly touched on the literary aspect of your novel. On this score it should be noted that because the novel is disjointed—even incoherent—in plot and composition, the impressions one gains from the various pages of the novel never cohere into a single, over-all picture but remain isolated. The novel contains many pages of first-class writing, particularly in those places where your perceptions and impressions of Russian nature are recorded with amazing accuracy and poetry. It also contains many clearly inferior pages, pages devoid of life and disfigured by didacticism. Such pages are particularly numerous in the second half of the novel.

However, we do not wish to dwell at any great length on this aspect of the matter, as we have already pointed out at the beginning of our letter: The crux of our argument with you has nothing to do with esthetic wrangling. You have written a novel that is distinctly and primarily a political sermon. You designed it as a work openly and completely placed at the service of specific political aims. And since that was the most important thing for you, it naturally became the principal object of our attention as well.

As unpleasant as it has been for us, we have had to call things by their proper names in our letter to you. We feel that your novel is profoundly unjust, that it lacks objectivity in its depiction of the revolution, the Civil War and the post-revolutionary years, that it is profoundly anti-democratic and alien to any conceivable understanding of the interests of the people. All this, by and large, stems from your position as a man who strives to show in his novel not only that the October Socialist Revolution had no positive importance in the history of our people and of mankind but that, on the contrary, it brought nothing but evil and misfortune.

As people whose position is diametrically opposed to yours, we naturally feel that publication of your novel in the magazine Novy Mir is out of the question. . . .

We are returning your manuscript of the novel "Doctor Zhivago."

DOCUMENT NO. 14

DE GAULLE TAKES POWER IN FRANCE, 1958*

France confronted many crises during the 1950s that led the nation to the brink of a military takeover of the democratic government. Foreign policy failures included the loss of Indo-China after years of fighting to retain that colony and, more recently, the negative outcome of the Suez War of 1956 against Egypt. Domestic problems during the Fourth Republic (1946–1958) revealed an unsatisfactory political environment that replaced governments on an average of nearly twice a year. These problems caused a loss of public confidence and jeopardized the fiscal stability of the state. Violence in the French colony of Algeria against rebels seeking independence brought the crisis to a head in 1958 as several French generals plotted a coup d'etat to replace the regime in Paris. The traumatized government turned to Charles de Gaulle for support. Famous as a general during World War II, de Gaulle had briefly led the nation at the end of the conflict. He agreed to take power in 1958 but demanded the granting of extensive powers to aid him in his efforts. This was given, and the result was the termination of the Fourth Republic, the writing of a new constitution, and the creation of the Fifth Republic. The powers of the executive branch were expanded, and de Gaulle became the first president under the new system. The excerpt below contains de Gaulle's comments to the National Assembly on June 1, 1958, when he outlined what the nation needed and the authority he required to deal with the current crisis.

γ   γ   γ

The rapidly accelerating degradation of the state, the immediate danger to French unity, Algeria in the throes of trials and emotions, Corsica suffering from a feverish contagion, opposing movements in Metropolitan France hourly whipping up their passions and, reinforcing their action, the Army, long tried by sanguinary and praiseworthy tasks but shocked by the lack of any real authority, our international position disparaged even within our alliances—such is the situation of our country. At this very moment, when so many opportunities, in so many directions, are offered to France, she finds herself threatened by disruption and perhaps even civil war.

* *Major Addresses, Statements and Press Conferences of General Charles de Gaulle: May 19, 1958—January 31, 1964* (New York, 1964), pp. 7–8.

It is in these circumstances that I offered my services to try, once again, to lead the country, the State, and the Republic to safety; and that, designated by the Chief of State, I have been led to ask the National Assembly to invest me with a heavy task. In order to perform this task, means are necessary.

If you invest this government, it will propose that you give it these means right away. It will ask you for full powers in order to be in a position to act with all the effectiveness, speed and responsibility demanded by the circumstances. It will ask you for these powers for a period of six months, hoping that at the end of this time—order having been re-established in the State, hope regained in Algeria, unity restored in the nation—it will be possible for the public powers to resume their normal course.

But what good would be a temporary remedy, a remedy of sorts, for a disastrous state of affairs unless we decided to eradicate the deep-seated cause of our troubles? This cause—the Assembly knows and the nation is convinced of it—is the confusion and, by the same token, the helplessness of constituted authority.

The Government which I shall form, provided I obtain your vote of confidence, will submit to you without delay a bill reforming Article 90 of the Constitution, thus enabling the National Assembly to give a mandate to the government to formulate and then propose to the country, through a referendum, the indispensable changes. In the explanatory statement which will be submitted to you at the same time as the text, the Government will specify the three principles which must be the basis of the republican regime in France and to which it pledges that its bill will conform: universal suffrage is the source of all power; the executive and legislative branches must be separate and apart so that the Government and the Parliament can, each for its own part and on its own responsibility, assume its full powers; the Government must be responsible to the Parliament.

Through the same constitutional reform, the country will be given a formal opportunity to organize the relations between the French Republic and the peoples associated with it. The Government will pledge itself to promote this new organization in the draft which it will put to the vote of the women and men of France.

Having received this double mandate, conferred on it by the National Assembly, the Government will be able to undertake the immense task which will have thus been defined. If I am to assume this double mandate, I shall first and foremost need your confidence. Then the Parliament must without delay—for events do not permit of any delay—enact into law the bills which will be submitted to it. These laws once passed, the Assemblies will adjourn until the date set for the opening of their next regular session. Thus the Government of the Republic, having been invested by the elected representatives of the nation and given, with extreme urgency, the means for action, can then be responsible for the unity, integrity, and independence of France.

DOCUMENT NO. 15

THE BERLIN CRISIS, 1958*

The geographic location of Berlin within Communist East Germany periodically made the city a focal point of controversy between the United States and the Soviet Union. The United States, Great Britain, and France had legal access to, and the right to be present in, West Berlin under signed agreements with Moscow. The Soviet blockade of West Berlin in 1948–1949 represented an early example of Cold War confrontation as the Russians sought to terminate the Western presence. Ten years after the earlier crisis, the Soviet leaders again targeted West Berlin, calling for the departure of the Western powers within six months. The following excerpts are from the American reply of December 31st, summarizing the legal status of West Berlin and the Western relationship with the city. The dispute subsided only to reappear in 1961 with the Communist decision to erect the Berlin Wall to physically divide the two parts of the city.

γ   γ   γ

The Government of the United States acknowledges the note which was addressed to it by the Government of the U.S.S.R. under date of November 27.

* *Department of State Bulletin*, 40 (January 19, 1959), pp. 79–81.

The note contains a long elaboration on the events which preceded and followed the last war. It attempts to portray the Western Powers— France, the United Kingdom and the United States—as supporters of Hitlerism as against the Soviet Union. This portrayal is in sharp contrast with the actual facts. . . .

The situation of Berlin of which the Soviet Government complains and which it considers abnormal is the result of the very nature of the German problem such as it has existed since 1945. When the empire of Hitler collapsed the Western Allies were in military possession of more than one-third of what subsequently was occupied by the Soviet authorities.

The Soviet Union was in possession of Berlin. On the basis of the agreements of September 12, 1944 and May 1, 1945, the Western Allies withdrew, thereby permitting a Soviet occupation of large parts of Mecklenburg, Saxony, Thuringia and Anhalt, and concurrently, the three Western Powers occupied the western sectors in Berlin, then an area of rubble.

The Soviet Union has directly and through its puppet regime—the so-called German Democratic Republic—consolidated its hold over the large area which the Western Allies relinquished to it. It now demands that the Western Allies should relinquish the positions in Berlin which in effect were the quid pro quo.

The three Western Powers are there as occupying powers and they are not prepared to relinquish the rights which they acquired through victory just as they assume the Soviet Union is not willing now to restore to the occupancy of the Western Powers the position which they had won in Mecklenburg, Saxony, Thuringia and Anhalt and which, under the agreements of 1944 and 1945, they turned over for occupation to the Soviet Union.

The agreements made by the Four Powers cannot be considered obsolete because the Soviet Union has already obtained the full advantage therefrom and now wishes to deprive the other parties of their compensating advantages. These advantages are binding upon all of the signatories so long as they have not been replaced by others following free negotiations. . . .

The United States Government cannot prevent the Soviet Government from announcing the termination of its own authority in the quadripartite regime in the sector which it occupies in the city of Berlin. On the other hand, the Government of the United States will not and does not, in any way, accept a unilateral denunciation of the accords of 1944 and 1945; nor is it prepared to relieve the Soviet Union from the obligations which it assumed in June, 1949. Such action on the part of the Soviet Government would have no legal basis, since the agreements can only be terminated by mutual consent. The Government of the United States will continue to hold the Soviet Government directly responsible for the discharge of its obligations undertaken with respect to Berlin under existing agreements. As the Soviet Government knows, the French, British and United States Governments have the right to maintain garrisons in their sectors of Berlin and to have free access thereto. Certain administrative procedures have been agreed with the Soviet authorities accordingly and are in operation at the present time. The Government of the United States will not accept a unilateral repudiation on the part of the Soviet Government of its obligations in respect of that freedom of access. Nor will it accept the substitution of the regime which the Soviet Government refers to as the German Democratic Government for the Soviet Government in this respect.

In the view of the Government of the United States, there can be no "threat" to the Soviet Government or the regime which the Soviet Government refers to as the German Democratic Republic from the presence of the French, British and United States garrisons in Berlin. Nor can there be any military threat from Berlin to the Soviet Government and this regime. The forces of the three Western Powers in Berlin number about ten thousand men. The Soviet Government, on the other hand, is said to maintain some three hundred and fifty thousand troops in Eastern Germany, while the regime which the Soviet Government refers to as the German Democratic Republic is understood also to maintain over two hundred thousand men under arms. In this circumstance, the fear that the Western troops in Berlin may "inflict harm" appears to be wholly unfounded. If Berlin has become a focus of international tension, it is because the Soviet Government has deliberately threatened to disturb the existing arrangements at present in force there, arrangements to which the Soviet Government is itself a party. The inhabitants of West Berlin have recently reaffirmed in a free vote their overwhelming approval and support for the existing status of that city. The continued protection of the freedom of more than two million people of West Berlin is a right and responsibility solemnly accepted by the three Western Powers. Thus the United States cannot consider any proposal which would have the effect of jeopardizing the freedom and security of these people. The rights of the Three Powers to remain in Berlin with unhindered communications by surface and air between that city and the Federal Republic of Germany are under existing conditions essential to the discharge of that right and responsibility. Hence the proposal for a so-called "free city" for West Berlin, as put forward by the Soviet Union, is unacceptable. . . .

In reality, the form of government in Berlin, the validity of which the Soviet Government attempts to contest today, is only one aspect, and not the essential one, of the German problem in its entirety. This problem, which has often been defined, involves the well-known questions of re-unification, European security, as well as a peace treaty. It has in the past been discussed without success in the course of numerous international meetings with the Soviets. The Government of the United States has always been and continues today to be ready to discuss it. . . .

Public repudiation of solemn agreements, formally entered into and repeatedly reaffirmed, coupled with an ultimatum threatening unilateral action to implement that repudiation unless it be acquiesced in within six months, would afford no reasonable basis for negotiations between sovereign states. The Government of the United States could not embark on discussions with the Soviet Union upon these questions under menace or ultimatum; indeed, if that were intended, the United States would be obliged immediately to raise a protest in the strongest terms. Hence, it is assumed that this is not the purpose of the Soviet note of November 27, and that the Soviet Government . . . is ready to enter into discussions in an atmosphere devoid of coercion or threats.

On this basis, the United States Government would be interested to learn whether the Soviet Government is ready to enter into discussions between the Four Powers concerned. In that event, it would be the ob-

ject of the Government of the United States to discuss the question of
Berlin in the wider framework of negotiations for resolution of the German problem as well as that of European security. The United States
Government would welcome the views of the Soviet Government at an
early date.

DOCUMENT NO. 16

THE COMMUNIST PARTY PROGRAM, 1961*

*The Communist Party of the Soviet Union, following the death of Joseph
Stalin in 1953, sought to present a more positive face to the public and world
in the aftermath of the repressive policies of the Stalin era and the ravages
resulting from the German invasion of the Soviet Union in World War II.
The nation, under the leadership of Nikita Khrushchev as First Secretary
of the Communist Party and also Prime Minister of the Soviet government,
called for a revised party program to update the existing version that had
served as the ideological basis of the party's role in prior decades. The new
program was adopted at the 22nd Congress of the Communist Party of the
Soviet Union on October 31, 1961. Not surprisingly, the document por-
trayed the present era and the goals of the future in highly optimistic terms,
as the following excerpt effectively illustrates. Actual outcomes showed that
the predicted results for the 1961–1980 period fell far short of the assurances.*

γ   γ   γ

THE TASKS OF THE COMMUNIST PARTY
OF THE SOVIET UNION IN BUILDING A
COMMUNIST SOCIETY

Communism—the Bright Future for All Mankind

The building of a communist society has become an immediate practical task for the Soviet people. The gradual development of socialism
into communism is an objective law; it has been prepared by the development of Soviet socialist society throughout the preceding period.

* *Programme of the Communist Party of the Soviet Union* (Moscow, 1961), pp. 59–62.

What is communism? Communism is a classless social system with one form of public ownership of the means of production and full social equality of all members of society; under it, the all-round development of people will be accompanied by the growth of the productive forces through continuous progress in science and technology; all the springs of co-operative wealth will flow more abundantly, and the great principle "From each according to his ability, to each according to his needs" will be implemented. Communism is a highly organised society of free, socially conscious working people in which public self-government will be established, a society in which labour for the good of society will become the prime vital requirement of everyone, a necessity recognised by one and all, and the ability of each person will be employed to the greatest benefit of the people.

A high degree of communist consciousness, industry, discipline, and devotion to the public interest are qualities typifying the man of communist society.

Communism ensures the continuous development of social production and rising labour productivity through rapid scientific and technological progress; it equips man with the best and most powerful machines, greatly increases his power over nature and enables him to control its elemental forces to an ever greater extent. The social economy reaches the highest state of planned organisation, and the most effective and rational use is made of the material wealth and labour reserves to meet the growing requirements of the members of society.

Under communism there will be no classes, and the socio-economic and cultural distinctions, and differences in living conditions, between town and countryside will disappear; the countryside will rise to the level of the town in the development of the productive forces and the nature of work, the forms of production relations, living conditions and the well-being of the population. With the victory of communism mental and physical labour will merge organically in the production activity of people. The intelligentsia will no longer be a distinct social stratum. Workers by hand will have risen in cultural and technological standards to the level of workers by brain.

Thus, communism will put an end to the division of society into classes and social strata, whereas the whole history of mankind, with the exception of its primitive period, was one of class society. Division into opposing classes led to the exploitation of man by man, class struggle, and antagonisms between nations and states.

Under communism all people will have equal status in society, will stand in the same relation to the means of production, will enjoy equal conditions of work and distribution, and will actively participate in the management of public affairs. Harmonious relations will be established between the individual and society on the basis of the unity of public and personal interests. For all their diversity, the requirements of people will express the sound, reasonable requirements of the fully developed person.

The purpose of communist production is to ensure uninterrupted progress of society and to provide all its members with material and cultural benefits according to their growing needs, their individual requirements and tastes. People's requirements will be satisfied from public sources. Articles of personal use will be in the full ownership of each member of society and will be at his disposal.

Communist society, which is based on highly organised production and advanced technology, alters the character of work, but it does not release the members of society from work. It will by no means be a society of anarchy, idleness and inactivity. Every able-bodied person will participate in social labour and thereby ensure the steady growth of the material and spiritual wealth of society. Thanks to the changed character of labour, its better technical equipment and the high degree of consciousness of all members of society, the latter will work willingly for the public benefit according to their own inclinations.

Communist production demands high standards of organisation, precision and discipline, which are ensured, not by compulsion, but through an understanding of public duty, and are determined by the whole pattern of life in communist society. Labour and discipline will not be a burden to people; labour will no longer be a mere source of livelihood—it will be a genuinely creative process and a source of joy.

Communism represents the highest form of organisation of public life. All production units and self-governing associations will be harmoniously united in a common planned economy and a uniform rhythm of social labour.

Under communism the nations will draw closer and closer together in all spheres on the basis of a complete identity of economic, political and spiritual interests, of fraternal friendship and co-operation.

Communism is the system under which the abilities and talents of free man, his best moral qualities, blossom forth and reveal themselves in full. Family relations will be freed once and for all from material considerations and will be based solely on mutual love and friendship.

In defining the basic tasks to be accomplished in building a communist society, the Party is guided by Lenin's great formula: "Communism is Soviet power plus the electrification of the whole country."

The C.P.S.U. being a party of scientific communism, proposes and fulfils the task of communist construction in step with the preparation and maturing of the material and spiritual prerequisites, considering that it would be wrong to jump over necessary stages of development, and that it would be equally wrong to halt at an achieved level and thus check progress. The building of communism must be carried out by successive stages.

In the current decade (1961–70) the Soviet Union, in creating the material and technical basis of communism, will surpass the strongest and richest capitalist country, the U.S.A., in production per head of population; the people's standard of living and their cultural and technical standards will improve substantially; everyone will live in easy circumstances; all collective and state farms will become highly productive and profitable enterprises; the demand of Soviet people for well-appointed housing will, in the main, be satisfied; hard physical work will disappear; the U.S.S.R. will have the shortest working day.

The material and technical basis of communism will be built up by the end of the second decade (1971–80), ensuring an abundance of material and cultural values for the whole population; Soviet society will come close to a stage where it can introduce the principle of distribution according to needs, and there will be a gradual transformation to one form of ownership—public ownership. Thus, a communist society will in the main be built in the U.S.S.R. The construction of communist society will be fully completed in the subsequent period.

The major edifice of communism is being erected by the persevering effort of the Soviet people—the working class, the peasantry and the intelligentsia. The more successful their work, the closer the great goal —communist society. . . .

DOCUMENT NO. 17

UNITED STATES STATEMENT ON BERLIN, 1961*

Periodic Berlin crises, as in 1948–1949 and 1958, reappeared in 1961 when the Soviet Union and the East German government again criticized the status of West Berlin and allied access to the city. President John Kennedy responded in a major radio and television report on July 25 about the growing seriousness of the situation and expressed American determination to protect the city. This included his request to Congress for larger military expenditures as well as substantial increases in military personnel by expanded use of the draft. Conditions deteriorated in the next few weeks, with the most tangible evidence being the construction by East German authorities of barbed wire and concrete barriers to divide West Berlin and East Berlin. This ended movement between the two segments of the city and further sealed off the West Berlin population. Although the Soviets and East Germans did not enter or physically damage West Berlin itself, a step which would have justified an immediate and direct American military response, the U.S. Government nonetheless immediately protested these hostile actions as exemplified in the erection of the "Berlin Wall." The following is the text of a Department of State note transmitted to the Soviet authorities on August 17th warning the Soviet Union against any interference with the status

* *Department of State Bulletin*, 40 (September 4, 1961), pp. 396–97.

of West Berlin as well as criticizing the construction of the barrier across the middle of the city.

γ   γ   γ

The Embassy of the United States presents its compliments to the Minister of Foreign Affairs and upon instructions of its Government has the honor to direct the most serious attention of the Government of the U.S.S.R. to the following.

On August 13, East German authorities put into effect several measures regulating movement at the boundary of the western sectors and the Soviet sector of the city of Berlin. These measures have the effect of limiting, to a degree approaching complete prohibition, passage from the Soviet sector to the western sectors of the city. These measures were accompanied by the closing of the sector boundary by a sizable deployment of police forces and by military detachments brought into Berlin for this purpose.

All this is a flagrant, and particularly serious, violation of the quadripartite status of Berlin. Freedom of movement with respect to Berlin was reaffirmed by the quadripartite agreement of New York of May 4, 1949, and by the decision taken at Paris on June 20, 1949, by the Council of the Ministers of Foreign Affairs of the Four Powers. The United States Government has never accepted that limitations can be imposed on freedom of movement within Berlin. The boundary between the Soviet sector and the western sectors of Berlin is not a state frontier. The United States Government considers that the measures which the East German authorities have taken are illegal. It reiterates that it does not accept the pretension that the Soviet sector of Berlin forms a part of the so-called "German Democratic Republic" and that Berlin is situated on its territory. Such a pretension is in itself a violation of the solemnly pledged word of the U.S.S.R. in the Agreement on the Zones of Occupation in Germany and the administration of Greater Berlin. Moreover, the United States Government cannot admit the right of the East German authorities to authorize their armed forces to enter the Soviet sector of Berlin.

By the very admission the East German authorities, the measures which have just been taken are motivated by the fact that an ever increasing number of inhabitants of East Germany wish to leave this territory. The reasons for this exodus are known. They are simply the internal difficulties in East Germany.

To judge by the terms of a declaration of the Warsaw Pact powers published on August 13, the measures in question are supposed to have been recommended to the East German authorities by those powers. The United States Government notes that the powers which associated themselves with the U.S.S.R. by signing the Warsaw Pact are thus intervening in a domain in which they have no competence.

It is to be noted that this declaration states that the measures taken by the East German authorities are "in the interests of the German peoples themselves". It is difficult to see any basis for this statement, or to understand why it should be for the members of the Warsaw Pact to decide what are the interests of the German people. It is evident that no Germans, particularly those whose freedom of movement is being forcibly restrained, think this is so. This would become abundantly clear if all Germans were allowed a free choice, and the principle of self-determination were also applied in the Soviet sector of Berlin and in East Germany.

The United States Government solemnly protests against the measures referred to above, for which it holds the Soviet Government responsible. The United States Government expects the Soviet Government to put an end to these illegal measures. This unilateral infringement of the quadripartite status of Berlin can only increase existing tension and dangers.

DOCUMENT NO. 18

THE SOVIET POSITION ON GERMANY AND WEST BERLIN, 1961*

Berlin continued to be a focal point of dispute in the Cold War, as it had been in 1948–49 and in 1958. In August 1961 the East German government constructed fortified barriers to surround and isolate the population of

---

* *Foreign Relations of the United States 1961–1963* (Washington, 1996), VI (*Kennedy-Khrushchev Exchanges*), pp. 29–35.

West Berlin, and the infamous "Wall" illustrated the confrontational nature of the East–West split. Soon after, Nikita Khrushchev wrote President John Kennedy proposing that a "peace" treaty be signed to confirm the boundaries of the West German and East German states. He also proposed that West Berlin become an international city, a step that would remove it as part of the territory of West Germany and also terminate U.S., British and French treaty rights there. Kennedy rejected the Russian proposal, but Khrushchev reiterated the same ideas in messages to the president in 1962. The following is a portion of a longer communication from Khrushchev to Kennedy on September 29, 1961, presenting his views of the German and Berlin topic. He made no comparable suggestion for East Berlin's status. This proposal shows the methods and arguments of the Soviet leader during a precarious and tense period of European history.

γ   γ   γ

You will agree with me, Mr. President, that the present international situation and its tension can hardly be assessed as a simple arithmetical sum total of unresolved issues. After all, the series of measures and counter-measures aimed at strengthening the armaments of both sides which have already been put into effect by our Governments in connection with the aggravation of the German question cannot be disregarded. I do not want here to engage in an argument as to who is right or wrong in the matter. Let us leave this aside for the time being. The main thing is that events are unfortunately continuing to develop in the same unfavourable direction. Instead of confidence we are turning to an even greater aggravation. . . .

That is another important reason why the Soviet Union is now attaching such exclusive significance to the German question. . . . History will not be reversed and West Berlin will not be moved to the other side of the Elbe [River]. I do not doubt that, given good will and desire, the Governments of our countries could find a common language in the question of a German peace treaty. Naturally in the solution of that question it is necessary to proceed from the obvious fact, which even a blind man cannot fail to see, that there exist two sovereign German States. . . .

In signing a German peace treaty the States that participated in the war will have to unconditionally recognize the presently constituted frontiers of the German Democratic Republic [East Germany] and the Federal Republic of Germany [West Germany]. Under the peace treaty those frontiers would be legally formalized, I stress legally, because de facto they already exist and cannot be changed without a war. . . . I would think that the legal formalization of the state borders which have taken shape after World War Two equally meets the interests of both the U.S.S.R. and the United States. Thus the borders that have taken shape and presently exist between the two German States would be formalized as well.

There remains the question of West Berlin which must also be solved when a German peace treaty is concluded. From whatever side we approach the matter, we probably will not be able to find a better solution than the transformation of West Berlin into a free city. And we shall proceed towards that goal. If, to our regret, the Western Powers will not wish to participate in a German peace settlement and the Soviet Union, together with the other countries that will be prepared to do so, has to sign a treaty with the German Democratic Republic we shall nonetheless provide a free city status for West Berlin.

Your statements, Mr. President, as well as the statements of other representatives of Western Powers not infrequently show signs of concern as to whether freedom for the population of West Berlin will be preserved, whether it will be able to live under the social and political system of its own choosing, whether West Berlin will be safeguarded against interference and outside pressure. I must say we see no difficulties in creating such conditions, the more so since the assurance of the freedom and complete independence of West Berlin is also our desire, is also our concern. I declare this on behalf of the Soviet Government, and on behalf of the socialist countries allied with us which are interested in the solution of the German question. I wish to emphasize in particular that the German Democratic Republic and the Head of that State Walter Ulbricht are of the same opinion. I say this with full knowledge and in all responsibility. . . .

Frankly speaking it is hard to understand what such apprehensions are based on. I am convinced that the guarantees established under a peace treaty will be honored and observed by all the States which will have signed the Treaty. Furthermore the Soviet Union as a party to the German peace treaty will feel itself responsible for the fulfillment of all the clauses of that treaty, including the guarantees in respect to West Berlin.

But if it is the common desire that responsibility for the observance of the status of West Berlin should be entrusted to the Soviet Union we shall be ready to assume such a responsibility. I and my colleagues in the Government have not infrequently given thought to the way in which the role of the Soviet Union in guarantees for West Berlin could be implemented in practice. If we were simply to make a statement that the Soviet Union will in some special way guarantee the immunity of West Berlin, you will agree that this could prejudice the sovereign rights of the German Democratic Republic and the other countries [that are] parties to the peace treaty. In order to prevent that, in order not to prejudice the prestige of any States—whether your ally or ours—I believe the question should be solved in the way we have already proposed, namely that token contingents of troops of the United States, the United Kingdom, France and the Soviet Union, the four great Powers which participated in the war against Hitlerite Germany, should be left in West Berlin. In my view that is the sole possibility. Naturally such a system should be introduced not for all time but for a specific period. Evidently an appropriate status for the deployment of the troops of the four Powers in West Berlin would then have to be devised which would be subject to the approval of the other countries [that are] signatories of the peace treaty.

Given every desire, we could find no other solution which to any greater degree would strengthen confidence in the reliability of guarantees for West Berlin. If you have any ideas of your own on this score we are ready to consider them. Of course, such alternatives are also conceivable as the deployment in West Berlin of troops from neutral countries or United Nations troops. I have repeatedly expressed and now reaffirm our agreement to such a solution. We also agree to the establishment of the United Nations Headquarters in West Berlin which would in that case become an international city.

It goes without saying that the occupation regime in West Berlin must be eliminated. Under the allied agreements [signed in 1945] occupation is a temporary measure and, indeed, never in history has there been a case of occupation becoming a permanent institution. But sixteen years have already elapsed since the surrender of Germany. For how long then is the occupation regime to be preserved?

A more stable status should be created for West Berlin than existed under the occupation. If the occupation regime has lived out its time and has become a source of strife among States it means the time has come to discard it. It has completely exhausted itself, has become a burden in relationships among nations and does not meet the interests of the population of West Berlin itself. The transformation of West Berlin into a free city will create a far more durable basis for its independent existence than the regime of occupation. Furthermore the grounds for collisions among States which are generated by the preservation of the occupation regime will disappear.

Of course, no one can be satisfied with half-measures which superficially would seem to erase from the surface differences among States while in effect they would be preserving them under cover and driving them in deeper. What use would there be if we barely covered up this delayed action landmine with earth and waited for it to explode. Indeed, no, the countries which are interested in consolidating peace must render the landmine completely harmless and tear it out of the heart of Europe.

The representatives of the United States sometimes declare that the American side is not advancing its concrete proposals on the German question because the Soviet Union allegedly is not striving for agreed solutions and wants to do everything by itself regardless of what other States may say. It is hard for me to judge how far such ideas really tell on the actions of the United States Government, but they are based on a profoundly mistaken assessment of the position of the Soviet Union. The United States Government can easily verify that, if it wishes to introduce its own constructive proposals at the negotiations on a peaceful settlement with Germany incorporating the question of West Berlin.

I am closely following the meetings of our Minister of Foreign Affairs Andrei A. Gromyko with the Secretary of State of the United States Mr. Dean Rusk. I do not know how you will react to this idea, but it seems to me that it would be useful to broaden contacts between our Governments on the German question. If the United States Government, like the Soviet Government, is searching for understanding and is ready to devise conditions for peace with Germany which would be acceptable for both sides and would not affect the interests or the prestige of any State I believe it could be arranged that you and I would appoint appropriate representatives for private meetings and talks. Those representatives would elaborate for us the contours of an agreement which we could discuss before coming to a peace conference where a decision on the question of a peace treaty with Germany will be taken. . . .

The non-aligned countries addressed messages to you, Mr. President, and to myself. They suggested that we meet to discuss outstanding problems. You gave a positive reply to that appeal. We too reacted favourably to the initiative of the neutrals. I believe a meeting between us could be useful and, given the desire of both sides, could culminate in the adoption of positive decisions. Naturally such a meeting would have to be well prepared through diplomatic or other confidential channels. And when preliminary understanding is reached, you and I could meet at any place in order to develop and formalize the results of such an understanding. This would undoubtedly be met with great satisfaction by all nations. They would see in that step an important contribution to the settlement of existing differences, to the consolidation of peace. The positive results of such a meeting would generate confidence that all issues can be solved peacefully by negotiations.

We are proposing that a German peace treaty be signed not only to eliminate the vestiges of World War Two, but also to clear the way for the elimination of the state of "cold war" which can at any moment bring our countries to the brink of a military collision. We want to clear the way for the strengthening of friendly relations with you and with all the countries of the world which espouse peaceful coexistence.

You, yourself, understand that we are a rich country, our expanse is boundless, our economy is on the upgrade, our culture and science are in their efflorescence. Acquaint yourself with the Program of our Party which determines our economic development for twenty years to come. This is indeed a grand and thrilling Program. What need have we of war? What need have we of acquisitions? And yet it is said that we want to seize West Berlin! It is ridiculous even to think of that. What would that give us? What would that change in the ratio of forces in the world arena? It gives nothing to anyone.

I often think how necessary it is for men who are vested with trust and great power to be inspired with the understanding of what seems to be an obvious truism, which is that we live on one planet and it is not in man's power—at least in the foreseeable future—to change that. . . . Therefore we must display concern for all of mankind, not to mention our own advantages, and find every possibility leading to peaceful solutions of problems. . . .

DOCUMENT NO. 19

THE "JUPITER" MISSILES DEAL, 1962*

The United States, in its "containment" policy toward the Soviet Union, provided military forces and armaments as part of NATO's defense shield. This included nuclear missiles (designated as "Jupiters") deployed in Turkey, a NATO ally. Soviet leaders periodically demanded their removal, as threatening and destabilizing in the Cold War environment. With the passage of time, this category became increasingly obsolete but still served Western interests in confronting Moscow. The Cuban Missile Crisis in the fall of 1962 again raised the Jupiter issue, when the United States demanded the removal of Soviet nuclear missiles from the Caribbean. Moscow again demanded the removal of the Jupiters in Turkey. President John Kennedy in fact favored their removal, but not as a quid pro quo for the missiles in Cuba. Secret conversations took place in October 1962 between Attorney General Robert Kennedy, the president's brother, and Soviet ambassador to the United States Anatoly Dobrynin. Their meetings primarily dealt with the Cuban crisis, but the two men also agreed that the Jupiters would be withdrawn at a later time. This step, however, was not to be described or interpreted as a quid pro quo for removing the missiles in Cuba. The following are excerpts of Dobrynin's October 27th message to his superiors in Moscow, describing how he and Kennedy reached an understanding on this subject. It was published in the Cold War International History Project Bulletin.

* http://cwihp.si.edu.

γ   γ   γ

Ciphered Telegram
TOP SECRET
Late tonight R. Kennedy invited me to come see him. We talked alone.
The Cuban crisis, R. Kennedy began, continues to quickly worsen. . . .

"In this regard," R. Kennedy said, "the president considers that a suitable basis for regulating the entire Cuban conflict might be the letter
N. S. Khrushchev sent on October 26 and the letter in response from
the President, which was sent off today to N. S. Khrushchev through
the U.S. Embassy in Moscow. The most important thing for us . . . is
to get as soon as possible the agreement of the Soviet government to
halt further work on the construction of the missile bases in Cuba and
take measures under international control that would make it impossible
to use these weapons.

"And what about Turkey?" I asked R. Kennedy.

"If that is the only obstacle to achieving the regulation I mentioned earlier, then the president doesn't see any insurmountable difficulties in re-
solving this issue," replied R. Kennedy. "The greatest difficulty for the
president is the public discussion of the issue of Turkey. Formally the
deployment of missile bases in Turkey was done by a special decision of
the NATO Council. To announce now a unilateral decision by the president of the USA to withdraw missile bases from Turkey—this would
damage the entire structure of NATO and the US position as the leader
of NATO. . . . In short, if such a decision were announced now it would
seriously tear apart NATO."

"However, President Kennedy is ready to come to agree on that question. . . . I think that in order to withdraw these bases from Turkey,"
R. Kennedy said, "we need 4–5 months. This is the minimum amount
of time necessary for the US government to do this, taking into account
the procedures that exist within the NATO framework. . . . However,
the president can't say anything public in this regard about Turkey."
R. Kennedy then warned that his comments about Turkey were extremely confidential; besides him and his brother, only 2–3 people know
about it in Washington.

"That's all that he asked me to pass on to N. S. Khrushchev," R. Kennedy said in conclusion. . . . He didn't even try to get into fights on various subjects, as he usually does, and only persistently returned to one topic: time is of the essence and we shouldn't miss the chance. After meeting with me he immediately went to see the president, with whom, as R. Kennedy said, he spends almost all his time now.

DOCUMENT NO. 20

THE CUBAN MISSILE CRISIS—THE SOVIET VIEW, 1962*

The Cold War reached a critical point about the proximity of military conflict and possible use of nuclear weapons in the Cuban missile crisis in the fall of 1962. Moscow's secret deployment of these missiles with nuclear warheads on the Caribbean nation seriously jeopardized the balance of power between the two super powers. On discovering the presence of these weapons, the United States moved promptly to take steps to deal with this destabilizing situation. John Kennedy's actions in late October to implement a naval quarantine are well known. Fortunately for both sides, the Soviet leadership agreed to withdraw the missiles. In return, the U.S. gave some assurances of its future policy toward Cuba. The following is a letter from Nikita Khrushchev to President Kennedy on November 20, 1962, several weeks after the imposition of the quarantine and Moscow's promise to remove these weapons. His statement provides the broader Soviet view of the situation and also summarizes the conditions that brought the crisis to an end. It also reveals other issues that remained to be resolved in the Soviet-American relationship.

γ   γ   γ

I have studied attentively your considerations which were forwarded through our Ambassador in Washington in the evening of November 15. I wish first of all to express satisfaction with regard to your statement that the United States is also interested in the achievement of a rapid progress in untying the Cuban knot. That is our great desire too.

* *Foreign Relations of the United States 1961–1963* (Washington, 1996), VI (*Kennedy-Khrushchev Exchanges*), pp. 215–22.

It is good that you have confirmed once again that the U.S. commitment to give assurance of non-invasion of Cuba, which was agreed upon in the exchange of messages on October 27 and 28 remains firm and clear. I fully share also the thought expressed by you about the necessity to act with caution, to take into consideration the position of others. Now when we speak of eliminating the remnants of the crisis this is as important as at any of its past stages.

I always believed and believe now that both of us are guided by the realization of the immense responsibility for the peaceful settlement of the crisis over Cuba being completed. The basis for such settlement already exists; the sides have achieved an agreement and have taken upon themselves certain obligations. It is precisely where we proceed from.

What have we agreed on? In brief our agreement has come to the following: The Soviet Union removes from Cuba rocket weapons which you called offensive and gives a possibility to ascertain this. The United States of American promptly removes the quarantine and gives assurances that there will be no invasion of Cuba, not only by the US but also by other countries in the Western Hemisphere. This is the essence of our agreement. . . .

We have dismantled and removed from Cuba all the medium range ballistic missiles to the last with nuclear warheads for them. All the nuclear weapons have been taken away from Cuba. The Soviet personnel who were servicing the rocket installations have also been withdrawn. . . . The U.S. Government was afforded the possibility to ascertain the fact that all 42 missiles that were in Cuba have really been removed.

What can be said in connection with the commitments of the American side? Proper consideration through the U.N of the commitment not to invade Cuba—and it is the main commitment of your side—so far is being delayed. The quarantine has not been lifted as yet. Permit me to express the hope that with receipt of this communication of mine you will issue instructions to the effect that the quarantine be lifted immediately with the withdrawal of your naval and other military units from the Caribbean area. Furthermore, your planes still continue to fly over the Cuban territory. It does not normalize the situation but aggravates it. And all this is taking place at the time when we have removed the missiles from Cuba, [and] have given you the possibility to ascertain it through appropriate observation. . . .

I will not conceal that lately I have to hear more and more often that we are too trustful with regard to the statements of the U.S. readiness to carry out its part of the agreement on Cuba and that the American side will under various pretexts evade the fulfillment of the obligations which it assumed. I do not want to believe this and I proceed from something different: the President has given his word and he will keep it as well as we keep our word. But in such an acute and delicate question which we face there cannot but exist the limits beyond which the trust begins losing its value if it is not being strengthened with practical steps towards each other. All this should be mutually taken into consideration to sooner crown with success our efforts in settling the conflict. . . .

Now about the conditions which you set forth with regard to carrying out the verification and measures of further observation. Yes, we really agreed to the effect that U.N. representatives could ascertain the removal from Cuba of rocket weapons which you called offensive. But we stipulated however that this question can be solved only with the consent of the Government of Cuba. We could not take an obligation for the Government of Cuba and your reference, Mr. President, that we allegedly took such an obligation, of course, does not reflect the real situation. I believe that you see for yourself the weakness of such a reference.

But what is the main thing in connection with the question of verification with regard to the missiles removed by us that is evaded in your communication? The main thing is that under agreement with you we gave you the possibility to carry out verification of the removal of our rockets in the open sea. We did that and that was an act of goodwill on our part. You will agree that we took this step in the circumstances when no promise had been made by us with regard to this matter in our messages. We did something more in comparison with what had been said by us in the message with regard to verification. . . . As a result the American side, as it itself so declared, had every opportunity to count the missiles put on our ships, to photograph them and to ascertain their removal.

Thus a way out was found and not a bad one, and the question of the verification must, of course, belong to the past. Now no one can doubt that we have carried out our commitment with regard to the dismantling and shipping of the missiles for Cuba which were a subject in our correspondence. The fact of the removal of those missiles has been officially confirmed also by the U.S. Department of Defense. . . .

You raise the question as to what to do next, how to ensure that those types of weapons on the removal of which we have agreed are not brought back to Cuba. I believe that with respect to non-introduction of such weapons in the future you and I do not have any differences. We are prepared to give firm assurances with regard to this matter. However, you speak not only about this. You now want some permanent supervision to be established, in Cuba or over Cuba. But where was it taken from that we gave our consent to permanent supervision? The question has never been put that way in the exchange of messages. And generally, how one can take as a normal thing an establishment, and without any reciprocity at that, of some permanent supervision over a sovereign state?

If we are are to show serious concern that no unexpected steps are taken on either side to the detriment of the other, then . . . the proposals of the U.N. Acting Secretary General U Thant on the so-called "presence of the U.N.," i.e. on establishing U.N. posts in the countries of the Caribbean area would meet this task. . . .

Let both of us agree, Mr. President, also that our representatives in New York be given at once the instructions to immediately proceed with working out an agreed document (or documents) that would formalize through the U.N. the commitments of the sides. As we see the matter this will require only a few days if, of course, all the sides want to have speediest liquidation of the aftermath of a tense and dangerous situation evolved in the Caribbean area, the situation that really brought humanity to the brink of thermonuclear war. . . .

Well, I think this answer of mine gives you not bad material for your statement at your press conference. However, I hope, Mr. President, that your statement will not be one-sided but will respond to mutual understanding of the situation with regard to immediate steps to remove the quarantine and to discontinue the flights of American planes over Cuba as well as with regard to the immediate formalizing through the U.N. of the commitments of the sides on the final liquidation of the crisis evolved [sic] in the Caribbean area.

In conclusion, I wish to stress that much time has already passed since an agreement was reached between us and it is not in the interests of our countries, not in the interest of peace to delay the fulfillment of the agreement that has been reached and the final settlement of the Cuban crisis. . . .

DOCUMENT NO. 21

THE AMERICAN VIEW OF THE CUBA SITUATION, 1962*

Document 20 is a message from Soviet Premier Nikita Khrushchev to President John Kennedy regarding the resolution of the Cuban Missile Crisis in the fall of 1962. The Soviet leader sent a further lengthy dispatch on this subject in December. The following is Kennedy's reply on December 14, 1962, giving the U.S. perspective on the issues and the efforts to resolve this tense and dangerous situation in a manner satisfactory to both sides. His letter also mentions other topics (such as Berlin, China, and a nuclear test ban) that reveal the range of international concerns that affected the great power relationship in the period.

γ   γ   γ

Dear Mr. Chairman: I was glad to have your message of December 11th and to know that you believe, as we do, that we have come to the final stage of the Cuba affair between us, the settlement of which will have significance for our future relations and for our ability to overcome other difficulties. I wish to thank you for your expression of appreciation of the understanding and flexibility we have tried to display.

* *Foreign Relations of the United States 1961–1963* (Washington, 1996), VI (*Kennedy-Khrushchev Exchanges*), pp. 231–33.

I have followed with close attention the negotiations of the final settlement of the Cuban question between your representative, Mr. Kuznetsov, and our representatives, Ambassador Stevenson and Mr. McCloy, in
New York. In these negotiations, we have tried to understand your position and I am glad to note that Mr. Kuznetsov has also shown effort
to understand our problems. It is clearly in the interest of both sides
that we reach agreement on how finally to dispose of the Cuban crisis.
To this end, Ambassador Stevenson and Mr. McCloy presented on
Wednesday a new draft of a joint statement which by now has certainly
reached you. I wish to assure you that it is our purpose to end this affair
as simply and clearly as possible.

You refer to the importance of my statements on an invasion of Cuba
and of our intention to fulfill them, so that no doubts are sown from the
very start. I have already stated my position publicly in my press conference of November 20th, and I am glad that this statement appears to
have your understanding; we have never wanted to be driven by the acts
of others into war in Cuba. The other side of the coin, however, is that
we do need to have adequate assurances that all offensive weapons are
removed from Cuba and are not reintroduced, and that Cuba itself com-
mits no aggressive acts against any of the nations of the Western Hemisphere. As I understand you, you feel confident that Cuba will not in
fact engage in such aggressive acts, and of course I already have your
own assurance about the offensive weapons. I myself should suppose
that you could accept our position—but it is probably better to leave
final discussion of these matters to our representatives in New York. I
quite agree that the larger part of the crisis has now been ended and we
should not permit others to stand in the way of promptly settling the
rest without further acrimony.

With regard to your reference to the confidential channels set up between us, I can assure you that I value them. I have not concealed from
you that it was a serious disappointment to me that dangerously mis-
leading information should have come through these channels before
the recent crisis. You may also wish to know that by an accident or misunderstanding one of your diplomats appears to have used a representative of a private television network as a channel to us. This is always

unwise in our country, where the members of the press often insist on printing at some later time what they may learn privately.

Because our systems are so different, you may not be fully familiar with the practice of the American press. The competition for news in this country is fierce. A number of the competitors are not great admirers of my Administration, and perhaps an even larger number are not wholly friendly to yours. Here in Washington we have 1200 reporters accredited to the White House alone, and thousands more in other assignments. It would be a great mistake to think that what appears in newspapers and magazines necessarily has anything to do with the policy and purpose of this government. I am glad to say that I have some friends among newspapermen, but no spokesmen.

But let me emphasize again that we do indeed value these confidential channels. I entirely share your view that some trust is necessary for leading statesmen of our two countries; I believe that it is important to build the area of trust whenever possible. I shall of course continue to hold and to express my convictions about the relative merits of our systems of government, and I will not be surprised if you do the same.

In particular, we have been very glad to have opportunities for private exchanges with and through Mr. Bolshakov, and I am sorry to learn that he is returning to Moscow. It is our impression that he has made a real effort to improve communications and understanding between our two governments, and we shall miss him very much.

I appreciate your writing me so frankly, and in return I have tried to be as straightforward, for I agree with you that only through such frank exchanges can we better understand our respective points of view. Partly for this reason I refrained in my last press conference from commenting on certain aspects of your speech before the Supreme Soviet with which you realize, of course, we could not agree.

We also are hopeful that once the Cuban crisis is behind us, we shall be able to tackle the other problems confronting us and to find the path to their solution.

I cannot refrain from commenting briefly on your reference to the German question, though I do not think that it would be useful in this message to expound our full position once again. But your suggestion that the interests of our two countries are toys in the hands of Chancellor Adenauer seems to me to miss entirely the true nature of the problem which confronts us in Central Europe. For here the rival interests of many states are involved—on your side as well as ours. If this is recognized, then I am confident that a way can be found which will accommodate these interests and which will lead to a peaceful settlement. I cannot quite agree with you that Mr. Rusk and Mr. Gromyko have settled everything on Berlin but one issue. They are skillful and experienced diplomats, but I do not think we should give them too much credit yet. Still it is quite true, as you say, that the main issue which seems to separate us on Berlin is that of the presence of allied troops in West Berlin. I am confident that if you could begin from an understanding of our position on this vital point, our chances of making progress would be greatly improved.

I look forward to receiving your confidential letter and proposals on the test ban question, and I think there is every reason to keep working on this problem. I hope that in your message on this subject you will tell me what you think about the position of the people in Peking on this question. It seems to me very important for both of us that in our efforts to secure an end to nuclear testing we should not overlook this area of the world. . . .

DOCUMENT NO. 22

DE GAULLE ON FRANCE AND THE UNITED STATES, 1963*

Charles de Gaulle became the President of France in 1958 and held that position until his resignation in 1969. One of his primary objectives in that period was to establish his nation as a recognized leader in European affairs

* Major Addresses, Statements and Press Conferences of General Charles de Gaulle: May 19, 1958–January 31, 1964 (New York, 1964), pp. 231–36.

and world politics. Examples of this objective included the development of its own nuclear weapons, recognition of Communist China, two vetoes of Britain's application to join the European Economic Community, termination of NATO's presence on French territory, and a cooling of relations with the United States especially during the Vietnam War. The following comments in a July 29, 1963 press conference provide a useful indication of his view on Franco-American relations. He puts part of the cause of this "widening" of the relationship on the United States itself, but De Gaulle also provides a broader historical context to justify France's determination to become more independent from its American ally.

γ   γ   γ

Question: Would you tell us, in your opinion, what are the effects of the recent international agreements which have just been signed in Moscow on the evolution of French-American relations?

Answer: There has been much agitation, particularly in the American press, in the last few months. I can tell you after my personal experience of nearly 25 years of public reactions in the United States, I am hardly surprised by the ups and downs of what it is customary there to call opinion. But, all the same, I must confess that recently the tone and the song, as regards France, have seemed rather excessive to me.

It is true that to judge this one has to take into account a certain tension which exists there and which is naturally caused by pressing domestic and foreign concerns, as well as by an electoral situation which is continually recurring. Needless to say I myself many times noted how this pounding was as useless as it was exaggerated. . . .

But I believe it useful to stress right away that this agitation by the press, political circles and more or less semiofficial bodies, which rages on the other side of the Atlantic and which naturally finds a ready echo in the various sorts of unconditional opponents, all of this agitation, I say, cannot alter in France what is fundamental as regards America. For us, the fundamental factors of French-American relations are friendship and alliance.

This friendship has existed for close on 200 years as an outstanding psychological reality in keeping with the nature of the two countries, special and reciprocal bonds maintained by the fact that among all the world powers France is the only one, with the exception, I should say, of Russia, with which the United States never exchanged a single cannon shot, while it is the only power without exception which fought at its side in three wars—the War of Independence and the First and Second World Wars—under conditions forever unforgettable.

For such a moral capital to be jeopardized would require infinitely serious and infinitely long dissension. There can be, there are, political divergencies between Paris and Washington. There is journalistic ill will. But it is not these divergencies, and it is not this journalistic ill will of the moment which can lead France to believe that the United States seeks to wrong her. Conversely, for the United States to imagine that France seeks to harm it would be a ridiculous absurdity. . . .

The Atlantic Alliance [North Atlantic Treaty Organization, established in 1949] is an elemental necessity, and it is obvious that in this respect the United States and France have a capital responsibility, the United States because it disposes of a nuclear armament without which the fate of the world would be rapidly settled and France because, whatever the present inferiority of its means, it is politically, geographically, morally, militarily essential to the coalition.

Thus if, once again, there are divergencies between Washington and Paris on the functioning of the organization of the Alliance, the Alliance itself—that is, the fact that in the event of a general war, France, with the means it has, would be at the side of the United States, and this I believe is mutual—is not in question except in the wanderings of those who make it their profession to alarm the good people by depicting each scratch as an incurable wound. Thus neither the French-American friendship nor the alliance could be questioned, nor are they. But it is true that in the presence of the problems now facing the two countries, their policies are not always in agreement. Moreover, there is nothing that is essential or fundamentally disturbing or even surprising. But we both must adapt ourselves to this new situation.

To my mind, the present differences are purely and simply the result of the intrinsic changes which took place in the last few years and which are continuing with regard to the absolute and relative situation of the United States and France. France had been materially and morally destroyed by the collapse of 1940 and by the capitulation of the Vichy people. Doubtless, the recovery achieved by the Resistance, at the sides of the Allies, gave her back, as though by a miracle, her integrity, her sovereignty and her dignity. But France came out of the ordeal greatly weakened in every respect. In addition, the inconsistency of the regime which she fell back upon prevented her from achieving her growth within and her rank without. Moreover, failing to adopt and to apply the decisions necessary with a view to decolonization, France's national development and international action were hampered by distant and fruitless struggles.

That is why, with regard to the United States—rich, active and powerful—she found itself in a position of dependence. France constantly needed its assistance in order to avoid monetary collapse. It was from America that she received the weapons for her soldiers. France's security was dependent entirely on its protection. With regard to the international undertakings in which its leaders at that time were taking part, it was often with a view to dissolving France in them, as if self-renouncement were henceforth its sole possibility and even its only ambition, while these undertakings in the guise of integration were automatically taking American authority as a postulate. This was the case with regard to the project for a so-called supranational Europe, in which France as such would have disappeared, except to pay and to orate; a Europe governed in appearance by anonymous, technocratic and stateless committees; in other words, a Europe without political reality, without economic drive, without a capacity for defense, and therefore doomed, in the face of the Soviet bloc, to being nothing more than a dependent of that great Western power, which itself had a policy, an economy and a defense—the United States of America.

But it happens that, since then, France's position has considerably changed. Her new institutions put her in a position to wish and to act. Her internal development brings her prosperity and gives her access to the means of power. She has restored her currency, her finances, her balance of trade, to such an extent that, from this standpoint, she no longer needs anyone, but to the contrary she finds herself receiving requests from many sides, and so, far from borrowing from others, particularly from the Americans, she is paying back her debts to them and even on occasion is granting them certain facilities. She has transformed into cooperation between States the system of colonization which she once applied to its African territories and, for the first time in a quarter of a century, she is living in complete peace.

France is modernizing her armed forces, is equipping them herself with materiel [sic] and is undertaking to endow herself with her own atomic force. She has cleared away the clouds which were surrounding and paralyzing the construction of Europe and is undertaking this great task on the basis of realities, beginning with the setting up of the economic community by giving, together with Germany, an example of the beginnings of political cooperation and by indicating that she wishes to be France within a Europe which must be European. Once again the national and international condition of our country resembles less and less what it used to be. How could the terms and conditions of her relations with the United States fail to be altered thereby? All the more so since the United States, on its side, as regards its own policies, is undergoing great changes which modify the character of hegemonic solidarity which, since the last World War, has marked its relations with France. . . .

But it remains that what happened in Moscow shows that the course followed by the policy of the United States is not identical with ours. With regard to defense, until recently the Americans, thanks to their nuclear weapons, were in a position to assure the free world almost complete protection, but they have lost this monopoly, while continuing at great expense to strengthen their power. Owing to the fact that the Russians also now have the wherewithal to destroy the world and particularly the new continent, it is quite natural that America is seeing its own survival as the principal objective in a possible conflict and is not considering the time, degree, terms and conditions of its nuclear intervention for the defense of other regions, particularly Europe, except in relation to this natural and primary necessity. This, moreover, is one of the reasons that France is equipping herself with her own atomic weapons. The result of this is that, as far as the French Government is concerned, important modifications are necessary with regard to the terms and conditions of our participation in the Alliance, since this organization has been built on the basis of integration, which today is no longer valid for us. . . .

DOCUMENT NO. 23

JOHN KENNEDY'S SPEECH IN BERLIN, 1963*

Cold War tensions between the superpowers periodically could be seen in divided Germany: the Berlin Blockade in 1948, another Berlin crisis in 1958, and the communist construction of the Berlin Wall in 1961 that was extended to separate the two German states, one communist and one democratic. President John Kennedy traveled to West Germany in the summer of 1963 to show his support for the government and people of the West German state. This included a memorable address on June 26 to the people of West Berlin, surrounded by communist East Germany, about their city that served as an inspiration for supporters of democracy.

γ   γ   γ

I am proud to come to this city as the guest of your distinguished Mayor [Willy Brandt, later the Chancellor of West Germany], who has symbolized throughout the world the fighting spirit of West Berlin, and I am proud to visit the Federal Republic with your distinguished Chancellor [Konrad Adenauer] who, for so many years, has committed Germany to democracy and freedom and progress, and to come here in the company of my fellow American, General Clay, who has been in this city during its great moments of crisis and will come again if ever needed.

Two thousands years ago the proudest boast was *"Civitas Romanus sum."* Today, in the world of freedom, the proudest boast is *"Ich bin ein Berliner."*

There are many people in the world who really don't understand, or say they don't, what is the great issue between the free world and the Com-

---

* *Department of State Bulletin*, 49 (July 22, 1963), pp. 124–25.

munist world. Let them come to Berlin. There are some who say that communism is the wave of the future. Let them come to Berlin. And there are some who say in Europe and elsewhere we can work with the Communists. Let them come to Berlin. And there are even a few who say that is it true that communism is an evil system but it permits us to make economic progress. *Lasst sie nach Berlin kommen.*

Freedom has many difficulties and democracy is not perfect, but we have never had to put a wall up to keep our people in, to prevent them from leaving us. I want to say, on behalf of my countrymen, who live many miles away on the other side of the Atlantic, who are far distant from you, that they take the greatest pride that they have been able to share with you, even from a distance, the story of the last 18 years. I know of no town, no city, that has been besieged for 18 years that still lives with the vitality and the force and the hope and the determination of the city of West Berlin. While the wall is the most obvious and vivid demonstration of the failures of the Communist system, for all the world to see, we take no satisfaction in it for it is, as your Mayor has said, an offense not only against history but an offense against humanity, separating families, dividing husbands and wives and brothers and sisters, and dividing a people who wish to be joined together.

What is true of this city is true of Germany—real, lasting peace in Europe can never be assured as long as one German out of four is denied the elementary right of free men, and that is to make a free choice. In 18 years of peace and good faith, this generation of Germans has earned the right to be free, including the right to unite their families and their nation in lasting peace, with good will to all people. You live in a defended island of freedom, but your life is part of the main.

So let me ask you, as I close, to lift your eyes beyond the dangers of today to the hopes of tomorrow, beyond the freedom merely of this city of Berlin, or your country of Germany, to the advance of freedom everywhere, beyond the wall to the day of peace with justice, beyond yourselves and ourselves to all mankind. Freedom is indivisible, and when one man is enslaved all are not free. When all are free, then we can look forward to that day when this city will be joined as one and this country and this great continent of Europe in a peaceful and hopeful glow. When that day finally comes, as it will, the people of West Berlin can take sober satisfaction in the fact that they were in the frontlines for almost two decades.

All free men, wherever they may live, are citizens of Berlin, and, therefore, as a free man, I take pride in the words *"Ich bin ein Berliner."*

DOCUMENT NO. 24

THE NUCLEAR TEST BAN TREATY, 1963*

The early 1960s increased East-West Cold War confrontation including the construction of the Berlin Wall (1961) and the Cuban Missile Crisis (1962). Large nuclear tests in this period further revealed the awesome power of the two superpowers. However, the governments in Moscow and Washington also adopted policies that showed that the two superpowers, although continuing to be rivals, might find common ground on strategic issues. A notable example is the agreement signed on July 25, 1963, to ban nuclear weapons tests in the atmosphere, in outer space and under water. Although this treaty did not totally ban nuclear testing, which could be detonated underground under the agreement, the administrations of President John F. Kennedy and Premier Nikita Khrushchev reduced the potential levels of radioactive fallout that caused serious health effects. Both nations adhered to the principles and procedures of the Test Ban Treaty for decades, even beyond the Soviet Union's collapse in 1991, showing that important international arms control treaties could be reached and implemented if the major parties were determined to do so. The United Kingdom also signed this treaty. France, possessing nuclear weapons, opted not to sign or support the treaty's prohibitions. A year later, in October 1964, China detonated a nuclear device, thus adding another state to the growing number of nations developing nuclear weapons.

γ   γ   γ

The Governments of the United States of America, the United Kingdom of Great Britain and Northern Ireland, and the Union of Soviet Socialist Republics, hereinafter referred to as the "Original Parties",

* U.S. Arms Control and Disarmament Agency, *Arms Control and Disarmament Agreements: Texts and History of Negotiations* (Washington, 1977), pp. 40–41.

Proclaiming as their principal aim the speediest possible achievement of an agreement on general and complete disarmament under strict international control in accordance with the objectives of the United Nations which would put an end to the armaments race and eliminate the incentive to the production and testing of all kinds of weapons, including nuclear weapons,

Seeking to achieve the discontinuance of all test explosions of nuclear weapons for all time, determined to continue negotiations to this end, and desiring to put an end to the contamination of man's environment by radioactive substances,

Have agreed as follows:

Article 1

1. Each of the Parties to this Treaty undertakes to prohibit, to prevent, and not to carry out any nuclear weapon test explosion, or any other nuclear explosion, at any place under its jurisdiction or control:

(a) in the atmosphere; beyond its limits, including outer space; or under water, including territorial waters or high seas; or

(b) in any other environment if such explosion causes radioactive debris to be present outside the territorial limits of the State under whose jurisdiction or control such explosion is conducted. It is understood in this connection that the provisions of this subparagraph are without prejudice to the conclusion of a treaty resulting in the permanent banning of all nuclear test explosions, including all such explosions underground, the conclusion of which, as the Parties have stated in the Preamble to this Treaty, they seek to achieve.

2. Each of the Parties to this Treaty undertakes furthermore to refrain from causing, encouraging, or in any way participating in, the carrying out of any nuclear weapon test explosion, or any other nuclear explosion, anywhere which would take place in any of the environments described, or have the effect referred to, in paragraph 1 of this Article.

Article II

1. Any Party may propose amendments to this Treaty. The text of any proposed amendment shall be submitted to the Depositary Governments which shall circulate it to all Parties to this Treaty. Thereafter, if requested to do so by one-third or more of the Parties, the Depositary

Governments shall convene a conference, to which they shall invite all the Parties, to consider such amendment.

2. Any amendment to this Treaty must be approved by a majority of the votes of all the Parties to this Treaty, including the votes of all of the Original Parties. The amendment shall enter into force for all Parties upon the deposit of instruments of ratification of all of the Original Parties.

Article III

1. This Treaty shall be open to all States for signature. Any State which does not sign this Treaty before its entry into force in accordance with paragraph 3 of this Article may accede to it any time. . . .

Article IV:

This Treaty shall be of unlimited duration. Each Party shall in exercising its national sovereignty have the right to withdraw from the Treaty if it decides that extraordinary events, related to the subject matter of this Treaty, have jeopardized the supreme interests of its country. It shall give notice of such withdrawal to all other Parties to the Treaty three months in advance.

DOCUMENT NO. 25

THE GULF OF TONKIN RESOLUTION, 1964*

America's economic and military involvement in the unstable conditions in Southeast Asia began during the Truman and Eisenhower administrations, and President Kennedy increased U.S. assistance to the government of South Vietnam in the early 1960s. The significant escalation of the U.S. military in a combat role began under President Lyndon Johnson, with the introduction of American land, sea, and air units to fight the communist forces of the Viet Cong and North Vietnam. One milestone in this growing involvement can be seen in the important "Gulf of Tonkin Resolution" that the Congress adopted on August 7, 1964. This resolution responded to what were identified at the time as North Vietnamese attacks on American naval vessels off the coast of North Vietnam. President Johnson asked Congress for authority to take any necessary steps to protect American interests in the area

* *Department of State Bulletin*, 51 (August 24, 1964), p. 268.

and to assist other regional governments seeking assistance. The vote in Congress showed overwhelming support of President Johnson: 88–2 in the Senate and 416–0 in the House of Representatives. Although not a formal declaration of war, this resolution became the primary congressional authority for expanding U.S. participation in the conflict. Congress rescinded the Tonkin Resolution in 1970, but only after America's massive involvement in the Vietnam War in which over 500,000 U.S. military personnel took part.

γ   γ   γ

To Promote the Maintenance of International Peace and Security in Southeast Asia.

Whereas naval units of the Communist regime in [North] Vietnam, in violation of the principles of the Charter of the United Nations and of international law, have deliberately and repeatedly attacked United States naval vessels lawfully present in international waters, and have thereby created a serious threat to international peace; and

Whereas these attacks are part of a deliberate and systematic campaign of aggression that the Communist regime in North Vietnam has been waging against its neighbors and the nations joined with them in the collective defense of their freedom; and

Whereas the Untied States is assisting the peoples of southeast Asia to protect their freedom and has no territorial, military or political ambitions in that area, but desires only that these peoples should be left in peace to work out their own destinies in their own way:

Now, therefore be it

Resolved by the Senate and House of Representatives of the United States of America in Congress assembled.

That the Congress approves and supports the determination of the President as Commander in Chief, to take all necessary measures to prevent further aggression.

Sec. 2.

The United States regards as vital to its national interest and to world peace the maintenance of international peace and security in southeast Asia. Consonant with the Constitution of the United States and the Charter of the United Nations and in accordance with the obligations under the Southeast Asia Collective Defense Treaty, the United States is, therefore, prepared, as the President determines, to take all necessary steps, including the use of armed force, to assist any member or protocol state of the Southeast Asia Collective Defense Treaty requesting assistance in defense of its freedom.

Sec. 3.

This resolution shall expire when the President shall determine that the peace and security of the area is reasonably assured by international conditions created by action of the United Nations or otherwise, except that it my be terminated earlier by concurrent resolution of the Congress.

DOCUMENT NO. 26

U.S. POLICY IN THE "SIX-DAY WAR," 1967*

Regional antagonism between Israel and its Arab neighbors resulted in periodic crises following the creation of the nation of Israel in 1948. Hostilities with Israel's neighbors broke out immediately in 1948, followed by wars in 1956 and 1967. The June 1967 war was the shortest of these conflicts, lasting approximately one week and having the name the "Six-Day War." Israel's primary opponent was Egypt, under Gamal Nasser, whose policies and actions in 1967 appeared to threaten Israel's security and existence. This included Nasser's demand in May for the removal of United Nations peacekeeping forces along the Egypt-Israel border, a new military defense pact with Jordan, and the prohibition of Israeli ships in the Strait of Tiran and the Gulf of Aqaba. Evidence of the buildup of military forces in Egypt, Syria, and Jordan, with modern weapons acquired from the Soviet Union, convinced the government of Prime Minister Levi Eshkol that an attack on Israel was imminent. The decision was made to take preemptive military action, which began on June 5, with quick and decisive Israeli victories on all fronts and the occupation of extensive territory, including the West Bank, East Jerusalem, the Golan Heights, and the Sinai Peninsula, of its Arab neighbors. Hostilities ended by June 10, as the several combatants agreed to a U.N. resolution to suspend military operations. The following is a portion of a June 6th speech to the United Nations Security Council by the U.S. representative, expressing his government's efforts to bring hostilities to an end.

* *American Foreign Policy: Current Documents, 1967* (Washington, 1969), pp. 508–510.

γ   γ   γ

In the resolution just adopted the Security Council, acting in the exercise of its responsibilities under the charter, has issued a clear call for an end to the hostilities in the Near East. This resolution is a first step on the road back toward peace. It carries the full authority of the United Nations. It is now the duty of all the parties concerned to comply fully and promptly with the terms of this resolution. It is equally the duty of every member of the United Nations to support the implementation of the resolution by the full weight of its influence.

The resolution itself, as all members of the Council know, is the result of intensive political efforts here at the United Nations during the past 36 hours, under the leadership of our President and by various governments and their distinguished representatives here. It reflects a successful harmonizing of our respective points of view toward a single goal: to quench the flames of war in the Near East and to begin to move toward peace in the area.

This resolution, with its appeal for a cease-fire, calls for precisely the action which my delegation has been urging since we met to consider the outbreak of hostilities yesterday morning. Indeed . . . it is consistent with the spirit in which we have approached every stage of the crisis. We have throughout supported every effort by our distinguished Secretary-General [of the United Nations] to maintain the peace in the area and sought to the best of our ability to exercise a restraining influence on the parties concerned. We have expressed willingness to join in the search for peace here in the United Nations and by our own diplomatic efforts as well.

Regrettably, our efforts and those of many others, including the Secretary General, to prevent a war ended in failure. When that was apparent, my Government considered that the first and foremost urgent step was to put an end to the tragic bloodshed by bringing an immediate halt to the hostilities. For this reason, the United States and other members in the past 36 hours vigorously urged as a first step the adoption of a resolution calling for an immediate cease-fire by all the governments concerned.

We deeply regret that so much time has been lost in the process. How-ever, it is gratifying that other members of the Council have now reached the same conclusion and that we can now issue a unanimous appeal to the parties to lay down their arms. It is our fervent hope that the Coun-cil's appeal will be immediately and fully complied with.

We believe that a cease-fire represents the urgent first step in restoring peace to the Near East. Once this is accomplished . . . my delegation believes that the Council should then turn its immediate attention to the other steps that will be required to achieve a more lasting peace. . . . In implementation of this policy directed to all countries in the Near East, when the fires have been dampened and tension reduced, we stand ready to join in efforts to bring a lasting peace to the area, in which cooperative programs for the economic and social development of all countries of the region would be an integral part. . . .

Mr. President [the chairman of the United Nations Security Council], in conclusion let me commend to every state the Council's resolution just adopted: Our duty now, as member states bound by the charter, is to place all the influence at the command of our respective governments behind the fulfillment of the decision unanimously arrived at by the Council. Properly carried out, this resolution will be a major step to-ward peace and security in the Near East and will provide a point of reference from which to resolve underlying problems in a sprit of justice and equity.

DOCUMENT NO. 27

PRESIDENT JOHNSON ON VIETNAM, 1968*

The United States took an active role in the Vietnam War during the 1960s, especially during the administration of Lyndon Johnson (President, 1963–1969). Large American land, sea, and air units joined the South Vietnam military in opposing the communist Viet Cong and North Vietnam

* *Public Papers of the Presidents of the United States: Lyndon Johnson, 1968–1969* (Wash-ington, 1970), Book 1, pp. 469–76.

forces in their efforts to conquer the Republic of South Vietnam. The Johnson administration adopted various strategies in this conflict in Southeast Asia, using a combination of extensive military operations including bombing North Vietnamese targets as well as offering to negotiate a settlement with the enemy. As American casualties and military expenditures increased, and lacking solid evidence that the enemy could be decisively resisted, segments of the U.S. public and Congress questioned America's continued participation in the conflict. The following excerpts are from a televised speech of President Johnson on March 31, 1968, in which he described the objectives of U.S. involvement and current efforts to reach a resolution of the war. He also made the unexpected announcement that he would not seek reelection in 1968.

γ   γ   γ

Good evening, my fellow Americans:

Tonight I want to speak to you of peace in Vietnam and Southeast Asia. No other question so preoccupies our people. No other dream so absorbs the 250 million beings who live in that part of the world. No other goal motivates American policy in Southeast Asia.

For years, representatives of our Government and others have traveled the world—seeking to find a basis for peace talks. Since last September, they have carried the offer that I made public at San Antonio. That offer was this: That the United States would stop its bombardment of North Vietnam when that would lead promptly to productive discussions— and that we would assume that North Vietnam would not take military advantage of our restraint.

Hanoi denounced this offer, both privately and publicly. Even while the search for peace was going on, North Vietnam rushed their preparations for a savage assault on the people, the government, and the allies of South Vietnam. Their attack—during the Tet holidays [January 1968]—failed to achieve its principal objectives. It did not collapse the elected government of South Vietnam or shatter its army—as the Communists had hoped. It did not produce a "general uprising" among the people of the cities as they had predicted. The Communists were unable to maintain control of any of the more than 30 cities that they attacked. And they took very heavy casualities. . . .

The Communists may renew their attack any day. They are, it appears, trying to make 1968 the year of decision in South Vietnam—the year that brings, if not final victory or defeat, at least a turning point in the struggle. This much is clear: If they do mount another round of heavy attacks, they will not succeed in destroying the fighting power of South Vietnam and its allies. But tragically, this is also clear: Many men—on both sides of the struggle—will be lost. A nation that has already suffered 20 years of warfare will suffer once again. Armies on both sides will take new casualties. And the war will go on.

There is no need for this to be so. There is no need to delay the talks that could bring an end to this long and this bloody war. Tonight, I renew the offer I made last August—to stop the bombardment of North Vietnam. We ask that talks begin promptly, that they be serious talks on the substance of peace. . . . We are prepared to move immediately toward peace through negotiations. So tonight, in the hope that this action will lead to early talks, I am taking the first step to de-escalate the conflict. We are reducing—substantially reducing—the present level of hostilities. And we are doing so unilaterally, and at once.

Tonight, I have ordered our aircraft and our naval vessels to make no attacks on North Vietnam, except in the area north of the demilitarized zone where the continuing enemy buildup directly threatens allied forward positions and where the movements of their troops and supplies are clearly related to that threat. The area in which we are stopping our attacks includes almost 90 percent of North Vietnam's population, and most of its territory. Thus there will be no attacks around the principal populated areas, or in the food-producing areas of North Vietnam. . . . But I cannot in good conscience stop all bombing so long as to do so would immediately and directly endanger the lives of our men and our allies. Whether a complete bombing halt becomes possible in the future will be determined by events.

Our purpose in this action is to bring about a reduction in the level of violence that now exists. It is to save the lives of brave men—and to save the lives of innocent women and children. It is to permit the contending forces to move closer to a political settlement. . . . Now, as in the past, the United States is ready to send its representatives to any forum, at any time, to discuss the means of bringing this ugly war to an end. . . .

I call upon President Ho Chi Minh to respond positively, and favorably, to this new step toward peace. But if peace does not come now through negotiations, it will come when Hanoi understands that our common resolve is unshakable, and our common strength is invincible. Tonight, we and the other allied nations are contributing 600,000 fighting men to assist 700,000 South Vietnamese troops in defending their little country.

Our presence there has always rested on this basic belief: The main burden of preserving their freedom must be carried out by them—by the South Vietnamese themselves. We and our allies can only help to provide a shield behind which the people of South Vietnam can survive and can grow and develop. On their efforts—on their determination and resourcefulness—the outcome will ultimately depend. That small, beleaguered nation has suffered terrible punishment for more than 20 years. I pay tribute again tonight to the great courage and endurance of its people. . . . Its people maintain their firm determination to be free of domination by the North. . . .

Last week President Thieu ordered the mobilization of 135,000 additional South Vietnamese. He plans to reach . . . a total military strength of more than 800,000 men. To achieve this, the Government of South Vietnam started the drafting of 19-year-olds on March 1st. On May 1st, the Government will begin the drafting of 18-year-olds. . . . All men in the South Vietnamese armed forces have had their tours of duty extended for the duration of the war, and reserves are now being called up for immediate active duty. . . .

We shall accelerate the re-equipment of South Vietnam's armed forces —in order to meet the enemy's increased firepower. This will enable them progressively to undertake a larger share of combat operations against the Communist invaders. On many occasions I have told the American people that we would send to Vietnam those forces that are required to accomplish our mission there. So, with that as our guide, we have previously authorized a force level of approximately 525,000.

Some weeks ago—to help meet the enemy's new offensive—we sent to Vietnam about 11,000 additional Marine and airborne troops. . . . In order that these forces may reach maximum combat effectiveness, the

Joint Chiefs of Staff have recommended to me that we should prepare to send—during the next 5 months—support troops totaling approximately 13,500 men. A portion of these men will be made available from our active forces. The balance will come from reserve component units which will be called up for service.

The actions that we have taken since the beginning of the year
—to re-equip the South Vietnamese forces,
—to meet our responsibilities in Korea, as well as our responsibilities in Vietnam,
—to meet price increases and the costs of activating and deploying reserve forces,
—to replace helicopters and provide the other military supplies we need, all of these actions are going to require additional expenditures. The tentative estimate of those additional expenditures is $2.5 billion in this fiscal year, and $2.6 billion in the next fiscal year. . . .

I cannot promise that the initiative that I have announced tonight will be completely successful in achieving peace any more than the 30 others that we have undertaken and agreed to in recent years. But it is our fervent hope that North Vietnam, after years of fighting that have left the issue unresolved, will now cease its efforts to achieve a military victory and will join with us in moving toward the peace table. . . . As Hanoi considers its course, it should be in no doubt of our intentions. It must not miscalculate the pressures within our democracy in this election year.

We have no intention of widening this war. But the United States will never accept a fake solution to this long and arduous struggle and call it peace. No one can foretell the precise terms of an eventual settlement. Our objective in South Vietnam has never been the annihilation of the enemy. It has been to bring about a recognition in Hanoi that its objective—taking over the South by force—could not be achieved. . . .

So tonight I reaffirm the pledge that we made at Manila—that we are prepared to withdraw our forces from South Vietnam as the other side withdraws its forces to the north, stops the infiltration, and the level of violence thus subsides. . . .

But let it never be forgotten: Peace will come also because America sent her sons to help secure it. It has not been easy—far from it. During the past 4 1/2 years, it has been my fate and my responsibility to be Commander in Chief. I have lived—daily and nightly—with the cost of this war. I know the pain that it has inflicted. I know, perhaps better than anyone, the misgivings that it has aroused. Throughout this entire, long period, I have been sustained by a single principle: that what we are doing now, in Vietnam, is vital not only to the security of Southeast Asia, but it is vital to the security of every American.

Surely we have treaties which we must respect. Surely we have commitments that we are going to keep. Resolutions of the Congress testify to the need to resist aggression in the world and in Southeast Asia. But the heart of our involvement in South Vietnam—under three different Presidents, three separate administrations—has always been America's own security. And the larger purpose of our involvement has always been to help the nations of Southeast Asia become independent and stand alone, self-sustaining, as members of a great world community— at peace with themselves, and at peace with all others. With such an Asia, our country—and the world—will be far more secure than it is tonight.

I believe that a peaceful Asia is far nearer to reality because of what America has done in Vietnam. I believe that the men who endure the dangers of battle—fighting there for us tonight—are helping the entire world avoid far greater conflicts, far wider wars, far more destruction, than this one. The peace that will bring them home someday will come. Tonight I have offered the first in what I hope will be a series of mutual moves toward peace. . . .

Finally, my fellow Americans, let me say this. . . . The ultimate strength of our country and our cause will lie not in powerful weapons or infinite resources or boundless wealth, but will lie in the unity of our people. This I believe very deeply. Throughout my entire public career I have followed the personal philosophy that I am a free man, an American, a public servant, and a member of my party, in that order always and only. For 37 years in the service of our Nation, first as a Congressman, as a Senator, and as Vice President, and now as your President, I have put the unity of the people first. I have put it ahead of any divisive partisanship. . . .

There is division in the American house now. There is divisiveness among us all tonight. And holding the trust that is mine, as President of all the people, I cannot disregard the peril to the progress of the American people and the hope and the prospect of peace for all peoples. . . . Believing this as I do, I have concluded that I should not permit the Presidency to become involved in the partisan divisions that are developing in this political year. With America's sons in the fields far away, with America's future under challenge right here at home, with our hopes and the world's hopes for peace in the balance every day, I do not believe that I should devote an hour or a day of my time to any personal partisan causes or to any duties other than the awesome duties of this office—the Presidency of your country. Accordingly, I shall not seek, and I will not accept, the nomination of my party for another term as your President. . . .

DOCUMENT NO. 28

FRENCH STUDENT DEMANDS, 1968*

The year 1968 was a unsettled period in the United States and several European nations. Public opposition to the Vietnam War, racial unrest in cities, the assassination of leading figures as Martin Luther King Jr., and student activism on university campuses, created tensions and occasional violence. In France, student frustration over academic curricula, crowded classrooms, and other educational grievances led to demonstrations in Paris, Nanterre and other cities. Students sought the assistance of other groups, such as labor unions, to pressure the authorities to meet their objectives. They also opposed the dominating leadership of Charles de Gaulle as the President of France. The following statement of the National Union of French Students (UNEF) outlines its frustrations, concerns and objectives. It shows the militant leftist ideological tone of the student movement in opposing the authori-

* *The French Student Revolt* by Hervé Bourges (New York: Hill & Wang, 1968). Originally published in French as La Révolte Etudiants. Copyright © 1968 by Editions du Seuil. Reprinted by permission of Georges Borchardt, Inc., for the Editions du Seuil. Pp. 84–88.

ties and the middle class features of French society. By the end of the year, university authorities promised reforms would be adopted but the changes fell short of the sweeping goals that many students demanded. When President De Gaulle resigned in 1969 after his proposal for reforming regional government was defeated in a national referendum, many students rejoiced at the news. Note: the word "faculty" or "faculties" has a different usage in American education when the term indicates course instructors. It refers in European higher education to organized curricular disciplines such as law, medicine, etc.

γ γ γ

Given the growth of the students' and workers' movement in Paris and the provinces and the results of the first debates in the faculties, the UNEF national executive regards it as its duty today to draw up a preliminary report and to put forward some proposals so as to reinitiate discussion and action in all French universities. One phenomenon, at any rate, is irreversible: the radical challenge to the university is inseparable from a challenge to the established authorities; in other words, from now on the struggle has moved onto the political terrain.

As new perspectives open before the movement that the students unleashed (the occupation of the factories by the workers), we must fight every attempt to slow down the movement, whether by restricting it to purely academic aims or by conceiving the union of workers and students as limited to the Sorbonne courtyard [the University of Paris]. That is why we must take part in the dynamic movement of social challenge, particularly by advancing the demand potential where it first emerged, in the universities. It is crucial to propose objectives that correspond to this analysis.

We now have four essential aims to propose to the student movement:
1. the immediate installation of real student power in the faculties with the right to veto any decision taken;
2. conditional on the first point, university and faculty autonomy;
3. the extension of the struggle to all those sectors that disseminate the ruling ideology, that is, the media;
4. a real union of workers' and peasants' struggles by posing the problem of the same type of challenge to the power of the authorities in business and professional structures.

These four essential points are necessary conditions for the resolution of other problems (the examinations; selection; political and trade-union freedom in faculties, schools and elsewhere).

1. Student Power

Whether the instrument is a critical university, student-dominated commissions, or a total change in faculty committees, it is crucial that the student movement retains control of all decisions taken in the university. Whatever structures for debate with the base are set up, only a student veto will enable all decisions taken to be put into practice, and prevent integration. This demand must be put into practice immediately, and it alone justifies continuing the strike. But we know that this type of power can only be temporary in a capitalist society.

2. University Autonomy

Without student power this autonomy is a trap since it amounts to giving power to the mandarins who govern us. On the other hand, without autonomy, student power is a trap, since government and administration would retain considerable means of control. Autonomy means that every decision taken by students in liaison with teachers will be applicable immediately.

3. Extension of the Struggle to Every Ideological Sector

The bourgeoisie is trying to drown the movement in the channels of communication, so we must use the same channels, on the contrary, to make our actions known and understood. This means that anything disseminated that plays into the hands of the authorities must be fought: whether on the air (the ORTF and outlying stations) or in the press. No paper must come out if it is printing false news. This action should be carried out in close alliance with journalists and printing workers. Similarly, the youth clubs and *maisons de la culture*, the theaters and the whole artistic section should join the battle for the creation of a new type of popular culture.

4. Liaison of the Workers' and Students' Struggles

The fall of the existing authorities can only be achieved if the workers themselves lead the struggle. This means that the main force for social transformation remains the working class. The workers must take their fate into their own hands and attack the power of the management forthwith. On our part, this presupposed systematic participation in the discussions that take place in the working class, to convey our point of view, not to give lectures. Inversely, every student-controlled university must be open to the workers for every discussion.

Thus clarified, these four points will allow us to act on the situation and realize our other demands:

1. The boycott of traditional examinations that only serve to eliminate those students who are the victims of an educational failure; a first synthesis of our discussions allows us to formulate the following principles:

(a) There can be no question of making students pay for challenging the examination system. This means that they must not lose the benefits of their year, nor must the examinations discriminate against the militants who have been fighting while others stayed quietly at home, or against wounded students as opposed to healthy ones. Given that the attack on examinations is linked to a total change in the education system, this means that any discussion on the assessment of knowledge must be subordinate to it. In the present circumstances it is crucial that there is student control of any examination procedure or other method of degree allocation; alteration of the content of possible tests in certain fields; control of every decision by the students.

(b) There can be no question of letting examinations and national competitions take their normal form. We propose that the CAPES [Certificate of Professional Aptitude for Higher Education] competition be changed into an examination: this means that the pre-established quota of places should be ignored; on the baccalaureate: the baccalaureate cannot be allowed to take its traditional form. As a minimum, we propose that school students should have powers of control, and that all candidates should take the oral examination.

2. Political and trade-union freedom exists in the faculties. It must be extended to the campuses (under student power with veto), to the *grandes écoles* and to the schools. On this point the UNEF not only declares itself in solidarity with the CALs [Leninist Action Committees], but also solemnly declares that it will take part in the struggle for the recognition of the CALs in the schools and for the their absolute freedom of expression and action.

3. No selection at university entrance or for any courses of higher education. Given that a total change of the education system is an absolutely priority, we reject any selection whatsoever.

What is to be done immediately?

1. It is crucial to continue basic discussions in all fields and at all levels. But from now on the UNEF calls on its militants to seize control of university administration for the students. If discussions with teachers are still necessary, a veto on all decisions is the only valid guarantee. As a function of the balance of forces, the control to be installed can only be given to the struggle committees, strike committees, or action committees which have really led the action in the last fortnight. Where the balance of forces is not so favorable, we must resort to parallel structures (critical universities, etc.) so that we can maintain enough pressure to disrupt the functioning of the traditional university. Though it is applicable in the present circumstances, this line may change according to the evolution of the balance of forces.

2. Proclamation of autonomy must be demanded forthwith. But this proclamation must not be made unless the first point (the veto) has been obtained, with all the necessary guarantees to prevent autonomy leading to a reinforcement of the conservative and technocratic teaching fractions.

3. The battle for communications must be conducted in every university town. This means that no local paper must come out unless it is doing its job correctly and reporting our struggles. Together with the printing workers, we should organize demonstrations, occupations of the buildings, distribution boycotts, etc. In the cultural sector, we and young workers can begin the battle to transform the activities of youth clubs and *maisons de la culture* into something more combative (occupations, initiation of political discussions, etc.). In other sectors of cultural life, we can look forward to interventions in alliance with those artists who have taken up a stand against bourgeois culture.

4. Occupation of the universities by the workers has already begun. Our role is that of a megaphone in a campaign of political explanation, to prevent the government or the reaction cutting the student struggle off from the workers' struggles. So UNEF militants should take part in the meetings and demonstrations decided on by the workers, and we should regard such participation as a priority.

This set of proposals is thrown open to the free discussions that have been going on in the universities for several days.   The UNEF National Executive

DOCUMENT NO. 29

THE NUCLEAR NON-PROLIFERATION TREATY, 1968*

Nuclear weapons during the Cold War not only grew in size, awesome power, and numbers, but the states possessing those destructive devices also grew. By the mid-1960s five nations were nuclear powers: China, France, Great Britain, the Soviet Union, and the United States. Other states established research programs that eventually might add them to the list. This led to efforts to reach an international agreement designed to prevent or reduce the spread of nuclear weapons information, technology, or materials that might be used for this purpose. Negotiations to achieve this goal successfully concluded in 1968, with the signing ceremony taking place jointly in Washington, London, and Moscow on July 1. When the treaty went into effect on March 5, 1970, 100 nations had signed the agreement.

γ   γ   γ

The States concluding this Treaty, hereinafter referred to as the "Parties to the Treaty",

Considering the devastation that would be visited upon all mankind by a nuclear war and the consequent need to make every effort to avert the danger of such a war and to take measures to safeguard the security of peoples,

Believing that the proliferation of nuclear weapons would seriously enhance the danger of nuclear war,

In conformity with resolutions of the United Nations General Assembly calling for the conclusion of an agreement on the prevention of wider dissemination of nuclear weapons,

Undertaking to cooperate in facilitating the application of International Atomic Agency safeguards on peaceful nuclear activities,

Expressing their support for research, development and other efforts to further the application, within the framework of the International Atomic Energy Agency safeguards system, of the principle of safeguarding effectively the flow of source and specific fissionable materials by use of instruments and other techniques at certain strategic points,

---

* U.S. Arms Control and Disarmament Agency, *Arms Control and Disarmament Agreements: Texts and History of Negotiations* (Washington, 1977), pp. 84–88.

Affirming the principle that the benefits of peaceful applications of nuclear technology, including any technological by-products which may be derived by nuclear-weapon States from the development of nuclear explosive devices, should be available for peaceful purposes to all Parties to the Treaty, whether nuclear-weapon or non-nuclear weapon States,

Convinced that, in furtherance of this principle, all Parties to the Treaty are entitled to participate in the fullest possible exchange of scientific information for, and to contribute alone or in cooperation with other States to, the further development of the applications of atomic energy for peaceful purposes,

Declaring their intention to achieve at the earliest possible date the cessation of the nuclear arms race and to undertake effective measures in the direction of nuclear disarmament,

Urging the cooperation of all States in the attainment of this objective,

Recalling the determination expressed by the Parties to the 1963 Treaty banning nuclear weapon tests in the atmosphere, in outer space and under water in its Preamble to seek to achieve the discontinuance of all test explosions of nuclear weapons for all time and to continue negotiations to this end,

Desiring to further the easing of international tension and the strengthening of trust between States in order to facilitate the cessation of the manufacture of nuclear weapons, the liquidation of all their existing stockpiles, and the elimination from national arsenals of nuclear weapons and the means of their delivery pursuant to a treaty on general and complete disarmament under strict and effective international control,

Recalling that, in accordance with the Charter of the United Nations, States must refrain in their international relations from the threat or use of force against the territorial integrity or political independence of any State, or in any other manner inconsistent with the Purposes of the United Nations, and that the establishment and maintenance of international peace and security are to be promoted with the least diversion for armaments of the world's human and economic resources,

Have agreed as follows:

Article I

Each nuclear-weapon State Party to the Treaty undertakes not to transfer to any recipient whatsoever nuclear weapons or other nuclear explosive devices or control over such weapons or explosive devices directly, or indirectly; and not in any way to assist, encourage, or induce any non-nuclear weapon State to manufacture or otherwise acquire nuclear weapons or other nuclear explosive devices, or control over such weapons or explosive devices.

Article II

Each non–nuclear-weapon State Party to the Treaty undertakes not to receive the transfer from any transferor whatsoever of nuclear weapons or other nuclear explosive devices or of control over such weapons or explosive devices directly, or indirectly; not to manufacture or otherwise acquire nuclear weapons or other nuclear explosive devices; and not to seek or receive any assistance in the manufacture of nuclear weapons or other nuclear explosive devices.

Article III

Each non–nuclear-weapon State Party to the Treaty undertakes to accept safeguards, as set forth in an agreement to be negotiated and concluded with the International Atomic Energy Agency in accordance with the Statute of the International Atomic Energy Agency and the Agency's safeguards system, for the exclusive purpose of verification of the fulfillment of its obligations assumed under this Treaty with a view to preventing diversion of nuclear energy from peaceful uses to nuclear weapons or other nuclear explosive devices. Procedures for the safeguards required by this article shall be followed with respect to source or special fissionable material whether it is being produced, processed or used in any principal nuclear facility or is outside any such facility. The safeguards required by this article shall be applied on all source or special fissionable material in all peaceful nuclear activities within the territory of such State, under its jurisdiction, or carried out under its control anywhere. . . .

Article IV

1. Nothing in this Treaty shall be interpreted as affecting the inalienable right of all the Parties to the Treaty to develop research, production and use of nuclear energy for peaceful purposes without discrimination and in conformity with articles I and II of this Treaty.

2. All the Parties to the Treaty undertake to facilitate, and have the right to participate in, the fullest possible exchange of equipment, materials and scientific and technological information for the peaceful uses of nuclear energy. Parties to the Treaty in a position to do so shall also

cooperate in contributing alone or together with other States or international organizations to the further development of the applications of nuclear energy for peaceful purposes, especially in the territories of non-nuclear-weapon States Party to the Treaty, with due consideration for the needs of the developing areas of the world. . . .

Article VI

Each of the Parties to the Treaty undertakes to pursue negotiations in good faith on effective measures relating to cessation of the nuclear arms race at an early date and to nuclear disarmament, and on a treaty on general and complete disarmament under strict and effective international control. . . .

Article X

1. Each Party shall in exercising its national sovereignty have the right to withdraw from the Treaty if it decides that extraordinary events, related to the subject matter of the Treaty, have jeopardized the supreme interests of its country. It shall give notice of such withdrawal to all other Parties to the Treaty and to the United Nations Security Council three months in advance. Such notice shall include a statement of the extraordinary events it regards as having jeopardized its supreme interests.

2. Twenty-five years after the entry into force of the Treaty, a conference shall be convened to decide whether the Treaty shall continue in force indefinitely, or shall be extended for an additional fixed period or periods. This decision shall be taken by a majority of the Parties to the Treaty.

DOCUMENT NO. 30

THE "BREZHNEV DOCTRINE," 1968*

Soviet military forces, with other Warsaw Pact allies, invaded Czechoslovakia in August 1968 to suppress reform policies undertaken by the Czech Communist Party under Alexander Dubcek. This intervention policy, com-

* By permission of the City News Publishing Company. Leonid Brezhnev, "Socialist States: The Marxist-Leninist Policy," *Vital Speeches of the Day,* 35 (December 15, 1968), pp. 131–35.

monly known as the "Brezhnev Doctrine" since that time, cautioned other communist regimes that the Soviet Union might take similar action if any of them moved too far from Moscow's influence. The following excerpts are from a lengthy message Soviet leader Leonid Brezhnev delivered to a high level national meeting of the Polish Communist Party on November 13, 1968, a few months after the intervention in Czechoslovakia.

γ   γ   γ

Comrade Congress delegates, dear Comrades. It is a great pleasure for our delegation to convey on behalf of the Central Committee of the CPSU [Communist Party of the Soviet Union], on behalf of the thirteen and a half million Soviet Communists warm fraternal greetings to the 5th Congress of the Polish United Workers' Party; all Polish Communists! We wish successful and fruitful work to your congress. . . . The experience of the Polish United Workers' Party, its activity both inside the country and in the international arena, make a substantial contribution to the international experience of Communists. That is why the report of the Central Committee of the Polish United Workers' Party and the Congress documents are of great interest for all of us. . . .

Comrades, we live in a difficult, tempestuous and interesting time. The world revolutionary process, centering around the struggle of the two main social systems of our age, socialism and capitalism, is developing irrepressibly. We have already achieved very much in this world-wide struggle. . . .

The balance of forces on a world-wide scale continues tilting in favour of socialism and its allies. The might of the socialist camp is now such that the imperialists are afraid of a military rout in case of a direct confrontation with the main forces of socialism. Of course, as long as imperialism exists, one can in no way disregard the danger of war which imperialist policy is fraught with. However, it is a fact that the imperialists in the new conditions also increasingly resort to other, more perfidious, tactics. They are probing for weak links in the socialist front, pursue a course towards subversive ideological activity inside the socialist countries, seek to influence the economic development of those countries, seek to sow enmity, to drive a wedge between them, to encourage and fan nationalist sentiments and tendencies, seek to isolate separate socialist states in order to strangle them next one by one. . . . The experience of the development and struggle of socialist countries in these new conditions in the past few years, and specifically, the recent activisation of forces hostile to socialism in Czechoslovakia are another and forceful reminder to the Communists of socialist countries how important it is not to forget for a single moment about certain extremely essential and time-tested truths. . . .

Experience shows us most convincingly of what exceptional, it can be said, decisive importance for the successful building of socialism it is to safeguard and constantly strengthen the guiding role of the Communist Party as the most advanced, leading, organising and directing force in all social development under socialism. The Party, armed with Marxist-Leninist theory, expressing the will of the working class and all working people, is the decisive force in the struggle for socialism and communism. . . . It is not without reason that the enemies of socialism always select precisely the Communist Party as the first target for their attacks. It is not without reason that the revisionists of all shades, the carriers of bourgeois influence in the working class movement, invariably seek to soften up, weaken the Party, undermine its organising foundation—the Leninist principle of democratic centralism, [to] propagate weakening of Party discipline. . . .

From all this the Communists of the Soviet Union, and, we are convinced, the Communists of other fraternal countries, draw the clear-cut conclusion for themselves: it is imperative to strengthen the unity and cohesion of the Party by all efforts, to raise in every way its guiding role in the development of society, [and] improve the forms of its activity. . . . The interests of the defence of each socialist country, the interests of its economic, scientific and cultural advance, all this calls for broadest cooperation between the fraternal countries, the allround development of various contacts between them, genuine internationalism.

The main stake of imperialism in its struggle against us is exactly the stake on disuniting the socialist countries, calculation on weakening our unity. . . . It is clear to everyone that the successful construction of socialism in the difficult conditions of that country [a reference to East Germany] is inseverably linked with active support and solidarity on the part of the other socialist countries, with extensive economic cooperation, with our military alliance [the Warsaw Treaty Organization, commonly known as the "Warsaw Pact"].

The socialist states stand for strict respect for the sovereignty of all countries. We emphatically oppose interference into the affairs of any states, [or] violations of their sovereignty. At the same time the establishment and defence of the sovereignty of states which have embarked upon the road of building socialism is of particular significance for us, Communists. The forces of imperialism and reaction seek to deprive the people now of this, now of that socialist country of their sovereign right they have gained to ensure the prosperity of their country, the well-being and happiness of the broad mass of the working people through building a society free from any oppression and exploitation. . . .

It is common knowledge that the Soviet Union has done much for the real strengthening of the sovereignty and independence of the socialist countries. The CPSU has always advocated that each socialist country determine the specific forms of its development along the road of socialism with consideration for its specific national conditions. However, it is known, Comrades, that there are also common laws governing socialist construction, a deviation from which might lead to a deviation from socialism as such. And when the internal and external forces hostile to socialism seek to revert the development of any socialist country towards the restoration of the capitalist order, when a threat to the cause of socialism in that country, a threat to the security of the socialist community as a whole emerges, this is no longer only a problem of the people of that country but also a common problem, [a] concern of all socialist countries.

It goes without saying that such an action as military aid to a fraternal country to cut short the threat to the socialist order is an extraordinary, enforced step, it can be sparked off only by direct actions of the enemies of socialism inside the country and beyond its boundaries, actions creating a threat to the common interests of the camp of socialism. Experience shows that in present conditions the victory of the socialist order in this or that country can be regarded as final and the restoration of capitalism can be regarded as excluded only if the Communist Party, as the guiding force of society, firmly carries through a Marxist-Leninist policy in the development of all spheres of public life; only if the Party indefatigably strengthens the defence of the country, the defence of its revolutionary gains, if it maintains itself and propagates amidst the people vigilance with regard to the class enemy, irreconcilability to bourgeois ideology; only if the principle of socialist internationalism is being sacredly observed, the unity and fraternal solidarity with other socialist countries is being strengthened. . . .

The main thing is that even though they have differences on some questions or other, the Communist and Workers' Parties seek the ways and means to develop international relations and are striving to strengthen unity of their ranks on the basis of Marxism-Leninism. We, for our part, have always seen the usefulness of a comradely exchange of opinions and are ready for an open discussion of the existing questions between the Communist Parties. We are confident that it is precisely through strengthening of our contacts and cooperation that the problems that arise will be solved in the interests of unity of the international communist movement. And this is natural for we have the joint ideological basis, Marxism-Leninism, the common enemy, imperialism, and the common goal, the victory of communism.

The situation calls for rallying the fraternal Parties to pass over to a more powerful offensive on imperialism. The immortal watchword of our movement "Workers of All Countries, Unite!" today resounds with renewed vigour for the Communists. . . . Long live the Polish United Workers' Party, the vanguard of the Polish working people that leads the country along the socialist road! May the unbreakable friendship between the peoples of Poland and the Soviet Union flourish forever! Long live communism!

DOCUMENT NO. 31

NOBEL PEACE PRIZE FOR WILLY BRANDT, 1971*

Cold War conditions in Europe following the Second World War divided the continent between the Soviet-dominated Eastern regions and the NATO alliance in the West. Germany, separated into two nations in 1949, became a focal point for periodic Cold War confrontations. Occasionally, opportuni-

* By permission of the Norwegian Nobel Institute.

ties appeared or were created to reduce tensions between the nuclear superpowers and their allies. A notable example can be seen in the efforts of Willy Brandt, Chancellor of West Germany (1969–1974), whose policy of "Ostpolitik" ("opening to the East") sought to improve the relationship between his nation and Eastern Europe, notably East Germany and Poland, as well as the Soviet Union. This included diplomatic contacts and understandings with the East German government to allow some Germans to visit the other side of "the Wall," a state visit to Warsaw in which he expressed remorse and regret for the Nazi invasion and effects of the wartime occupation, and better relations with Moscow. For his continuing efforts to reduce confrontation, Willy Brandt was selected as the recipient of the 1971 Nobel Peace Prize. The following is a portion of the Nobel Committee's award citation as delivered by the President of the Nobel Committee, Mrs. Aase Lionaes.

γ   γ   γ

This year, the Nobel Committee of the Norwegian Storting [Parliament] have chosen to give the Peace Prize to a man for whom the ideal of peace has been a guiding-star throughout his active political career— Federal Chancellor Willy Brandt. . . .

In 1966, the political situation in [West] Germany led to a coalition government between the two major parties, the Christian Democrats and the Social Democrats. In this government, Willy Brandt served as Foreign Secretary and Vice Chancellor. And it is from this new and wider political perspective that he is able to take the international initiatives on behalf of his government that led toward the present hope of international détente. This possibility of renewal and a more distinct formulation of [West] Germany's foreign policy goals became, of course, even greater in 1969 when Brandt was made Federal Chancellor. It was the beginning of a new chapter in Brandt's life and in the history of Germany. . . .

As Head of Government, Willy Brandt has not deviated from the principles of extending West European co-operation. On the contrary, he has added a new dimension to it, by stressing that a strong and co-operating Western Europe is a prerequisite to achieve a change form confrontation to co-operation between Eastern Europe and Western Europe. . . . Based on the strength and unity of West European economic and political co-operation, and with the support of the 15 NATO member countries, Willy Brandt's government now took up a more active policy of détente towards the Soviet Union and other East European countries. . . .

These concrete initiatives are specified in 4 clauses in the Government Declaration of October 28, 1969. Clause 1 deals with efforts to be taken to deepen and enlarge the European Economic Community and strengthen the political co-operation with it. Clause 2 speaks of a non-violence agreement with the Soviet Union. Clause 3 expresses the will to initiate talks with Poland with a view to normalizing the relations with this country. Clause 4 contains a declaration that the Government wishes to sign a non-proliferation treaty. . . .

With this first step, Brandt's government paved the way for a meaningful dialogue between East and West. With his expeditious mode of action, he contributed to the clarity of and the trust in the Federal Republic's will for détente. A policy of détente to successfully bring the peoples of Europe together requires both parties to step out of the trenches of the cold war. . . . Brandt's East European policy is an attempt to bury hatred and seek reconciliation across the mass graves of the war. How important it was for him personally to carry out this task of reconciliation is demonstrated by his kneeling by the Jewish memorial in the former ghetto of Warsaw.

The first concrete result of Brandt's efforts for relaxation in Germany's relations with the Soviet Union was the signing of a non-violence agreement in Moscow on August 12, 1970. In this agreement, it is established that all controversial issues shall be solved in a peaceful manner, and that peace only can be secured if both countries refrain from violating each other's borders. Both countries declared that they do not have territorial claims on other countries and that they would respect the integrity of all other countries within their present boundaries. The agreement also contained mutual wishes for more economic, technical and cultural co-operation. . . .

On December 7, 1970, shortly after the signing of the Moscow agreement, an agreement for normalizing the relations with Poland was signed. The most important part of this agreement was the Federal Republic's recognition of the western border of Poland, i.e., the Oder–Neisse line. Furthermore, it was agreed that the two countries would have no territorial claims on each other. . . . In a speech made in Warsaw to the German people, Brandt said among other things: "I am well aware of the fact that this is a difficult journey. It will be of importance for a future in peace. The Warsaw Agreement shall be the symbolic end of sufferings and sacrifices of an evil past. It shall build a bridge between countries and peoples. It shall open a way that leads to the reunion of families that live apart and to borders that separate less than before."

A condition by the government of the Federal Republic for submitting the two agreements to the parliament for ratification was, however, that an agreement be made between the four occupying powers to secure the connection of West Berlin to the Federal Republic of Germany. This condition seems to have been fulfilled by the Four–Power Agreement that was made on September 3 of this year. In this general agreement, the four occupying powers agree to refrain from threats to use instruments of force in Berlin and to solve all problems in a peaceful manner.

Movements between West Berlin and the Federal Republic have been facilitated, and the possibilities for the inhabitants of West Berlin to travel to East Berlin and the DDR [East Germany] are greater. The fact that the inhabitants of West Berlin will be able to visit their families behind "the Wall" is, from a humane point of view, of course one of the most important achievements. The agreement put a final end to an era where West Berlin was the place for confrontation between East and West; confrontations that have caused political crises and near-war conditions. Brandt made the following statement when interviewed by "Die Zeit" in November this year: "Of course, the Berlin agreements cannot solve all long-term problems for the city. This will only be possible when we have come substantially closer to a European peace order. 'The Wall' is still there, but it is less impenetrable."

It is the four problem areas that I have tried to outline here that are the essence of Willy Brandt's policy of co-operation and détente. This policy of his might pave the way for further initiatives to reduce tension in Europe. Willy Brandt himself mentions in an interview that there is hope for a mutual reduction in military forces as well as for de–escalation of armaments in Europe, especially in Central Europe. Let us hope that a development in this direction in Europe will lay the foundations for a global order of peace. . . .

Willy Brandt's . . . work for peace means possibilities for peoples of all countries to lead a dignified life without fear. What people want is to live in a Europe without separating walls and borders guarded by rockets, a Europe where . . . the branch of a rose bush is enough to designate a border. Willy Brandt's peace work has had a difficult starting-point. We have experienced one of the most barbaric wars in history. . . . I see a hope for the future in giving this year's Peace Prize to an active politician on the international arena. As such, he has a greater responsibility as well as greater possibilities of making a contribution that can subsequently bear the longed for fruits of peace. We can see for ourselves that Willy Brandt's policy of peace has brought thaw to the cold political climate, and this instills hopes for a new kind of peace for the frozen earth of Europe. . . .

The struggle for peace is a continuous process—it is a project that has to be worked at every day, over and over again. But people cannot live without hope and belief. Therefore, we shall hope and therefore we shall believe that Willy Brandt's gesture of reconciliation across the borders of old enemies will be interpreted in the spirit it was made. If these hopes are fulfilled, Willy Brandt will live on in our history as the great Peace and Reconciliation Chancellor of Germany.

DOCUMENT NO. 32

THE ABM TREATY, 1972*

The Soviet Union and the United States negotiated several important nuclear weapons treaties in the 1970s. While both sides continued the arms race and the potential for nuclear conflict remained, these complex agreements clarified and improved their relationship. Major objectives were a greater degree of predictability and avoidance of destabilizing the strategic balance

* U.S. Arms Control and Disarmament Agency, *Arms Control and Disarmament Agreements: Texts and History of Negotiations* (Washington, 1977), pp. 132–35.

during the Cold War. The first, the Anti-Ballistic Missile (ABM) treaty, was signed in Moscow on May 26, 1972 by U.S. President Richard Nixon and Communist Party General Secretary Leonid Brezhnev. Its primary provisions reduced the number of defensive missile sites to two areas that could be utilized in the event of a nuclear attack of ICBMs (intercontinental ballistic missiles). In 1974 the number was reduced to one ABM multi-missile complex. This accord did not include alternative methods of missile defense or other types of offensive weapons, but it served as the basis of another agreement signed at the same time that limited the number of long-range strategic weapons on each side.

γ   γ   γ

The United States of America and the Union of Soviet Socialist Republics, hereinafter referred to as the Parties,

Proceeding from the premise that nuclear war would have devastating consequences for all mankind,

Considering that effective measures to limit anti-ballistic missile systems would be a substantial factor in curbing the race in strategic offensive arms and would lead to a decrease in the risk of outbreak of war involving nuclear weapons,

Proceeding from the premise that the limitation of anti-ballistic missile systems, as well as certain agreed measures with respect to the limitation of strategic offensive arms, would contribute to the creation of more favorable conditions for further negotiations on limiting strategic arms,

Mindful of their obligations under Article VI of the [1968] treaty on the Non-Proliferation of Nuclear Weapons,

Declaring their intention to achieve at the earliest possible date the cessation of the nuclear arms race and to take effective measures toward reductions in strategic arms, nuclear disarmament, and general and complete disarmament,

Desiring to contribute to the relaxation of international tension and the strengthening of trust between States,

Have agreed as follows:

Article I

1. Each party undertakes to limit anti-ballistic missile (ABM) systems and to adopt other measures in accordance with the provisions of this Treaty.

2. Each party undertakes not to deploy ABM systems for a defense of the territory of its country and not to provide a base for such a defense, and not to deploy ABM systems for defense of an individual region except as provided for in Article III of this Treaty.

Article II

1. For the purpose of this Treaty, an ABM system is a system to counter strategic ballistic missiles or their elements in flight trajectory, currently consisting of:

(a) ABM interceptor missiles, which are interceptor missiles constructed and deployed for an ABM role, or of a type tested in an ABM mode;

(b) ABM launchers, which are launchers constructed and deployed for launching ABM interceptor missiles; and

(c) ABM radars, which are radars constructed and deployed for an ABM role, or of a type tested in an ABM mode.

2. The ABM system components listed in paragraph 1 of this Article include those which are:

(a) operational;

(b) under construction;

(c) undergoing testing;

(d) undergoing overhaul, repair or conversion; or

(e) mothballed.

Article III

Each Party undertakes not to deploy ABM systems or their components except that:

(a) within one ABM system deployment area having a radius of one hundred and fifty kilometers and centered on the Party's national capital, a Party may deploy: (1) no more than one hundred ABM launchers and no more than one hundred ABM interceptor missiles at launch sites, and (2) ABM radars within no more than six ABM radar complexes, the area of each complex being circular and having a diameter of no more than three kilometers; and

(b) within one ABM system deployment area having a radius of one hundred and fifty kilometers and containing ICBM silo launchers, a Party may deploy: (1) no more than one hundred ABM launchers and no more than one hundred ABM interceptor missiles at launch sites, (2) two large phased-array ABM radars comparable in potential to corresponding ABM radars operational or under construction on the date of signature of the Treaty in an ABM system deployment area containing ICBM silo launchers, and (3) no more than eighteen ABM radars each having a potential less than the potential of the smaller of the above-mentioned two large phased-array ABM radars.

Article IV

The limitations provided for in Article III shall not apply to ABM systems or their components used for development or testing, and located within current or additionally agreed test ranges. Each Party may have no more than a total of fifteen ABM launchers at test ranges.

Article V

1. Each Party undertakes not to develop, test, or deploy ABM systems or components which are sea-based, air-based, space-based, or mobile land-based.
2. Each Party undertakes not to develop, test, or deploy ABM launchers for launching more than one ABM interceptor missile at a time from each launcher, nor to modify deployed launchers to provide them with such a capability, nor to develop, test, or deploy automatic or semi-automatic or other similar systems for rapid reload of ABM launchers. . . .

Article VII

Subject to the provisions of this Treaty, modernization and replacement of ABM systems or their components may be carried out.

Article VIII

ABM systems or their components in excess of the numbers or outside the areas specified in this Treaty, as well as ABM systems of their components prohibited by this Treaty, shall be destroyed or dismantled under agreed procedures within the shortest possible agreed period of time.

Article IX

To assure the viability and effectiveness of this Treaty, each Party undertakes not to transfer to other States, and not to deploy outside its national territory, ABM systems or their components limited by this Treaty. . . .

Article XI

The Parties undertake to continue active negotiations for limitations on strategic offensive arms.

Article XII

1. For the purpose of providing assurance of compliance with the provisions of this Treaty, each Party shall use national technical means of verification at its disposal in a manner consistent with generally recognized principles of international law.

2. Each Party undertakes not to interfere with the national technical means of verification of the other Party operating in accordance with paragraph 1 of this Article.

3. Each Party undertakes not to use deliberate concealment measures which impede verification by national technical means of compliance with the provisions of this Treaty. This obligation shall not require changes in current construction, assembly, conversion, or overhaul procedures.

Article XIII

1. To promote the objectives and implementation of the provisions of this Treaty, the Parties shall establish promptly a Standing Consultative Committee. . . .

Article XIV

1. Each Party may propose amendments to this Treaty. Agreed amendments shall enter into force in accordance with the procedures governing the entry into force of this Treaty.

2. Five years after entry into force of this Treaty, and at five-year intervals thereafter, the Parties shall together conduct a review of this Treaty.

Article XV

1. This treaty shall be of unlimited duration.

2. Each Party shall, in exercising its national sovereignty, have the right to withdraw from this Treaty if it decides that extraordinary events related to the subject matter of this Treaty have jeopardized its supreme interests. It shall give notice of its decision to the other Party six months prior to withdrawal from the Treaty. Such notice shall include a statement of the extraordinary events the notifying Party regards as having jeopardized its supreme interests. . . .

DOCUMENT NO. 33

THE INTERIM AGREEMENT (SALT I), 1972*

U.S. and Soviet efforts to reduce the threat of possible nuclear conflict emerged out of the superpower confrontations of the 1960s in Southeast Asia, the Middle East, and Central Europe, as well as the nuclear arms race that produced even more destructive weapons. By 1969, Washington and Moscow had begun negotiations to limit the numbers and size of long-range strategic nuclear weapons, the Intercontinental Ballistic Missiles (ICBMs), capable of reaching between the two nations. These complex negotiations eventually resulted in a major nuclear arms treaty known as "SALT I" (Strategic Arms Limitation Treaty I), signed in the spring of 1972. It included two major components: the ABM or anti-ballistic missile treaty (described in document 32), and a ceiling on American and Soviet strategic offensive weapons for five years ("Interim Agreement"). The following is the text of the "Interim Agreement" signed in Moscow on May 26, 1972, by President Richard Nixon and General Secretary of the Communist Party Leonid Brezhnev. Despite its limited duration, the agreement is an example of nuclear arms control efforts. A more comprehensive nuclear treaty ("SALT II"), signed in 1979, was never ratified.

γ   γ   γ

The United States of America and the Union of Soviet Socialist Republics, hereinafter referred to as the Parties,

Convinced that the Treaty on the Limitation of Anti-Ballistic Missile Systems and this Interim Agreement on Certain Measures with Respect to the Limitation of Strategic Offensive Arms will contribute to the creation of more favorable conditions for active negotiations on limited strategic arms as well as to the relaxation of international tension and the strengthening of trust between States,

Taking into account the relationship between strategic offensive and defensive arms,

Mindful of their obligations under Article VI of the Treaty on the Non-Proliferation of Nuclear Weapons,

Have agreed as follows:

---

* U.S. Arms Control and Disarmament Agency, *Arms Control and Disarmament Agreements: Texts and History of Negotiations* (Washington, 1977), pp. 138–39.

Article I

The parties undertake not to start construction of additional fixed land-based inter-continental ballistic missiles (ICBM) launchers after July 1, 1972.

Article II

The Parties undertake not to convert land-based launchers for light ICBMs, or for ICBMs of older types deployed prior to 1964, into land-based launchers for heavy ICBM's of types deployed after that time.

Article III

The Parties undertake to limit submarine-launched ballistic missile (SLBM) launchers and modern ballistic missile submarines to the numbers operational and under construction on the date of signature of this Interim Agreement, and in addition to launchers and submarines constructed under procedures established by the Parties as replacements for an equal number of ICBM launchers of older types deployed prior to 1964 or for launchers on older submarines.

Article IV

Subject to the provisions of this Interim Agreement, modernization and replacement of strategic offensive ballistic missiles and launchers covered by this Interim Agreement may be undertaken.

Article V

1. For the purpose of providing assurance of compliance with the provisions of this Interim Agreement, each Party shall use national technical means of verification at its disposal in a manner consistent with generally recognized principles of international law.

2. Each Party undertakes not to interfere with the national technical means of verification of the other Party operating in accordance with paragraph 1 of this Article.

3. Each Party undertakes not to use deliberate concealment measures which impede verification by national technical means of compliance with the provisions of this Interim Agreement. This obligation shall not require changes in current construction, assembly, conversion, or overhaul practices.

Article VI

To promote the objectives and implementation of the provisions of this Interim Agreement, the Parties shall use the Standing Consultative

Commission established under Article XIII of the Treaty on the Limitation of Anti-Ballistic Missile Systems in accordance with the provisions of that Article.

Article VII

The Parties undertake to continue active negotiations for limitations on strategic offensive arms. The obligations provided for in this Interim Agreement shall not prejudice the scope or terms of the limitation on strategic offensive arms which may be worked out in the course of further negotiations.

Article VIII

1. This Interim Agreement shall enter into force upon exchange or written notices of acceptance by each Party, which exchange shall take place simultaneously with the exchange of instruments of ratification of the Treaty on the Limitation of Anti-Ballistic Missile Systems.

2. This Interim Agreement shall remain in force for a period of five years unless replaced earlier by an agreement on more complete measures limiting strategic offensive arms. It is the objective of the Parties to conduct active follow-on negotiations with the aim of concluding such an agreement as soon as possible.

3. Each Party shall, in exercising its national sovereignty, have the right to withdraw from this Interim Agreement if it decides that extraordinary events related to the subject matter of this Interim Agreement have jeopardized its supreme interests. It shall give notice of its decision to the other Party six months prior to withdrawal from this Interim Agreement. Such notice shall include a statement of the extraordinary events the notifying Party regards as having jeopardized its supreme interests. . . .

DOCUMENT NO. 34

THE HELSINKI ACCORDS, 1975*

During the early 1970s, the United States and the Soviet Union entered a period of greater cooperation that came to be known as "détente." Several summit meetings between the leaders of both nations, and the signing of a number of agreements on various topics, illustrated the positive results of re-

* http://www.state.gov/www/global/arms/bureau.

ducing divisive issues and tensions on the European continent. A major example of this effort can be seen in negotiations between 1973 and 1975 held in Helsinki Finland as the conference site. Thirty-five European and North American nations participated in these talks that eventually led to a comprehensive treaty titled "Confidence and Security Building Measures" signed on August 1, 1975. A major element guaranteed the inviolability of national frontiers and the prohibition of intervention in other states. Human and civil rights also were a primary priority. The following are excerpts of the treaty, commonly known as the "Helsinki Accords."

γ   γ   γ

[The governments of Austria, Belgium, Bulgaria, Canada, Cyprus, Czechoslovakia, Denmark, Finland, France, East Germany, Greece, Holy See (Vatican), Hungary, Iceland, Ireland, Italy, Liechtenstein, Luxembourg, Malta, Monaco, Netherlands, Norway, Poland, Portugal, Romania, San Marino, Spain, Sweden, Switzerland, Turkey, Soviet Union, United Kingdom, United States, West Germany, and Yugoslavia]. . . .

Motivated by the political will, in the interest of peoples, to improve and intensify their relations and to contribute in Europe to peace, security, justice and cooperation as well as to rapprochement among themselves and with the other States of the world,

Determined, in consequence, to give full effect to the result of the conference and to assure, among their States and throughout Europe, the benefits deriving from those results and thus to broaden, deepen and make continuing and lasting the process of détente . . . have solemnly adopted the following. . . .

The participating States will respect each other's sovereignty, equality and individuality as well as all the rights inherent in and encompassed by its sovereignty, including in particular the right of every State to juridical equality, to territorial integrity and to freedom and political independence. They will also respect each other's right freely to choose and develop its political, social, economic and cultural systems as well as its right to determine its laws and regulations. . . .

The participating States will refrain in their mutual relations, as well as in their international relations in general, from the threat or use of force against the territorial integrity or political independence of any State, or in any other manner inconsistent with the purposes of the United Nations and with the present Declaration. No consideration may be invoked to serve to warrant resort to the threat of use of force in contravention of this principle. According, the participating States will refrain from any acts constituting a threat of force or direct or indirect use of force against another participating State. . . . No such threat or use of force will be employed as a means of settling disputes, or questions likely to give rise to disputes, between them. . . .

The participating States regard as inviolable all one another's frontiers as well as the frontiers of all States in Europe and therefore they will refrain now and in the future from assaulting those frontiers. Accordingly, they will also refrain from any demand for, or act of, seizure and usurpation of part or all of the territory of any participating State. . . .

The participating States will settle disputes among them by peaceful means in such a manner as not to endanger international peace and security, and justice. They will endeavor in good faith and a spirit of cooperation to reach a rapid and equitable solution on the basis of international law. For this purpose they will use such means as negotiation, enquiry, mediation, conciliation, arbitration, judicial settlement or other peaceful means of their own choice including any settlement procedure agreed to in advance of disputes to which they are parties. In the event of failure to reach a solution by any of the above peaceful means, the parties to a dispute will continue to seek a mutually agreed way to settle the dispute peacefully. . . .

The participating States will refrain from any intervention, direct or indirect, individual or collective, in the internal or external affairs falling within the domestic jurisdiction of another participating State, regardless of their mutual relations. They will accordingly refrain from any form of armed intervention or threat of such intervention against another participating State. . . .

The participating States will respect human rights and fundamental freedoms, including the freedom of thought, conscience, religion or belief, for all without distinction as to race, sex, language or religion. They will promote and encourage the effective exercise of civil, political, economic, social, cultural and other rights and freedoms all of which derive from the inherent dignity of the human person and are essential for his free and full development. . . .

The participating States on whose territory national minorities exist will respect the right of persons belonging to such minorities to equality before the law, will afford them the full protection for the actual employment of human rights and fundamental freedoms and will, in this manner, protect their legitimate interests in this sphere. . . .

By virtue of the principle of equal rights and self-determination of peoples, all peoples always have the right, in full freedom, to determine, when and as they wish, their internal and external political status, without external interference, and to pursue as they wish their political, economic, social and cultural development.

The participating States reaffirm the universal significance of respect for and effective exercise of equal rights and self-determination of peoples for the development of friendly relations among themselves as among all States; they also recall the importance of the elimination of any form of violation of this principle. . . .

They will endeavour, in developing their co-operation as equals, to promote mutual understanding and confidence, friendly and good-neighbourly relations among themselves, international peace, security and justice. They will equally endeavour, in developing their cooperation, to improve the well-being of peoples and contribute to the fulfilment of their aspirations through . . . the benefits resulting from increased mutual knowledge and from progress and achievement in the economic, scientific, technological, social, cultural and humanitarian fields. They will take steps to promote conditions favourable to making these benefits available to all. . . .

DOCUMENT NO. 35

REAGAN AND THE "EVIL EMPIRE," 1983*

The Cold War between the United States and the Soviet Union reached a new level of intensity by 1980, the year Ronald Reagan was elected president. Reagan's victory in part rested on his strong anti-communist outlook, a reputation he held for many years before coming to the presidency. Confrontations over the development and deployment of intermediate range nuclear missiles in Europe, the break-down of nuclear arms control negotiations, and the hostile rhetoric emanating from both capitals revealed the depths of the tension by the time Reagan took office. On March 8, 1983, the president spoke before the convention of the National Association of Evangelicals and used that opportunity to express his views on a number of topics including abortion and school prayer. He also described nuclear arms control issues such as a possible "freeze" on nuclear weapons. Reagan's speech became especially memorable for his criticism of communism, when he characterized the Soviet Union as the "evil empire." The following excerpts contain his critique of communism as compared to the democratic values of America.

γ   γ   γ

I'm pleased to be here today with you who are keeping America great by keeping her good. Only through your work and prayers and those of millions of others can we hope to survive this perilous century and keep alive this experiment in liberty, this last, best hope of man. . . .

There is sin and evil in the world, and we're enjoined by Scripture and the Lord Jesus to oppose it with all our might. Our nation, too, has a legacy of evil with which it must deal. The glory of this land has been its capacity for transcending the moral evils of our past. For example, the long struggle of minority citizens for equal rights, once a source of disunity and civil war, is now a point of pride for all Americans. We must never go back. There is no room for racism, anti-Semitism, or other forms of ethnic and racial hatred in our country. . . . But whatever sad episodes exist in our past, any objective observer must hold a positive view of American history, a history that has been the story of hopes

* *Public Papers of the Presidents of the United States: Ronald Reagan, 1983,* (Washington, 1984), Book 1, pp. 359–64.

fulfilled and dreams made into reality. Especially in this century, America has kept alight the torch of freedom, but not just for ourselves but for millions of others around the world.

And this brings me to my final point today. During my first press conference as President, in answer to a direct question, I pointed out that, as good Marxist-Leninists, the Soviet leaders have openly and publicly declared that the only morality they recognize is that which will further their cause, which is world revolution. I think I should point out I was only quoting Lenin, their guiding spirit, who said in 1920 that they repudiate all morality that proceeds from supernatural ideas—that's their name for religion—or ideas that are outside class conceptions. Morality is entirely subordinate to the interests of class war. And everything is moral that is necessary for the annihilation of the old, exploiting social order and for uniting the proletariat.

Well, I think the refusal of many influential people to accept this elementary fact of Soviet doctrine illustrates an historical reluctance to see totalitarian powers for what they are. We saw this phenomenon in the 1930's. We see it too often today. This doesn't mean we should isolate ourselves and refuse to seek an understanding with them. I intend to do everything I can to persuade them of our peaceful intent, to remind them that it was the West that refused to use its nuclear monopoly in the forties and fifties for territorial gain and which now proposes 50-percent cut in strategic ballistic missiles and the elimination of an entire class of land-based, intermediate-range nuclear missiles.

At the same time, however, they must be made to understand we will never compromise our principles and standards. We will never give away our freedom. We will never abandon our belief in God. And we will never stop searching for a genuine peace. But we can assure none of these things America stands for through the so-called nuclear freeze solutions proposed by some. The truth is that a freeze now would be a very dangerous fraud, for that is merely the illusion of peace. The reality is that we must find peace through strength.

I would agree to a freeze if only we could freeze the Soviets' global desires. A freeze at current levels of weapons would remove any incentives for the Soviets to negotiate seriously in Geneva and virtually end our chances to achieve the major arms reductions which we have proposed. Instead, they would achieve their objectives through the freeze.

A freeze would reward the Soviet Union for its enormous and unparalleled military buildup. It would prevent the essential and long overdue modernization of United States and allied defenses and would leave our aging forces increasingly vulnerable. And an honest freeze would require extensive prior negotiations on the systems and numbers to be limited and on the measures to ensure effective verification and compliance. And the kind of a freeze that has been suggested would be virtually impossible to verify. Such a major effort would divert us completely from our current negotiations on achieving substantial reductions.

A number of years ago, I heard a young father, a very prominent young man in the entertainment world, addressing a tremendous gathering in California. It was during the time of the cold war, and communism and our own way of life were very much on people's minds. And he was speaking to that subject. And suddenly, though, I heard him saying, "I love my little girls more than anything. . . . " And I said to myself, "Oh, no, don't. You can't—don't say that." But I had underestimated him. He went on: "I would rather see my little girls die now, still believing in God, than have them grow up under communism and one day die no longer believing in God."

There were thousands of young people in that audience. They came to their feet with shouts of joy. They had instantly recognized the profound truth in what he had said, with regard to the physical and the soul and what was truly important.

Yes, let us pray for the salvation of all of those who live in that totalitarian darkness—pray they will discover the joy of knowing God. But until they do, let us be aware that while they preach the supremacy of the state, declare its omnipotence over individual man, and predict its eventual domination of all peoples on the Earth, they are the focus of evil in the modern world.

It was C. S. Lewis who, in his unforgettable "Screwtape Letters," wrote: "The greatest evil is not done now in those sordid 'dens of crime' that Dickens loved to paint. It is not even done in concentration camps and labor camps. In those we see its final result. But it is conceived and ordered (moved, seconded, carried and minuted) in clear, carpeted, warmed, and well-lighted offices, by quiet men with white collars and cut fingernails and smooth-shaven cheeks who do not need to to raise their voice."

Well, because these "quiet men" do not "raise their voices," because they sometimes speak in soothing tones of brotherhood and peace, because, like other dictators before them, they're always making "their final territorial demand," some would have us accept them at their word and accommodate ourselves to their aggressive impulses. But if history teaches anything, it teaches that simple-minded appeasement or wishful thinking about our adversaries is folly. It means the betrayal of our past, the squandering of our freedom.

So, I urge you to speak out against those who would place the United States in a position of military and moral inferiority. . . . So, in your discussions of the nuclear freeze proposals, I urge you to beware of the temptation of pride—the temptation of blithely declaring yourselves above it all and label both sides equally at fault, to ignore the facts of history and the aggressive impulses of an evil empire, to simply call the arms race a giant misunderstanding and thereby remove yourself from the struggle between right and wrong and good and evil.

I ask you to resist the attempts of those who would have you withhold your support for our efforts, this administration's efforts, to keep America strong and free, while we negotiate real and verifiable reductions in the world's nuclear arsenals and one day, with God's help, their total elimination. While America's military strength is important, let me add here that I've always maintained that the struggle now going on for the world will never by decided by bombs or rockets, by armies or military might. The real crisis we face today is a spiritual one; at root, it is a test of moral will and faith. . . .

I believe we shall rise to the challenge. I believe that communism is another sad, bizarre chapter in human history whose last pages even now are being written. I believe this because the source of our strength in the quest for human freedom is not material, but spiritual. And because it knows no limitation, it must terrify and ultimately triumph over those who would enslave their fellow man. For in the words of Isaiah: "He giveth power to the faint; and to them that have no might He increased strength. . . . But they that wait upon the Lord shall renew their strength, they shall mount up with wings as eagles, they shall run and not be weary. . . . "

DOCUMENT NO. 36

THE INF TREATY, 1987*

Soviet-American relations began to improve in the mid-1980s, as Moscow and Washington looked for issues on which they could negotiate with greater chance of compromise and success. The rise to power of Mikhail Gorbachev as the new Soviet leader played an important role in this more cooperative relationship. A notable example of this effort can be seen in the Intermediate Nuclear Forces treaty signed in Washington, D.C. on December 8, 1987 by Gorbachev and U.S. President Ronald Reagan. The agreement provided for the phased removal and destruction of an entire category of nuclear weapons on both sides within three years, and the agreement represents the first time both governments had negotiated actual reductions of such devices.

The existence of this category of intermediate range weapons in the late 1970s and early 1980s had been a serious impediment to East-West relations, as both the United States and the Soviet Union had deployed these operational weapons on European territory. Their use in a nuclear war would have caused massive damage to that region, as well as potentially escalating such a crisis to an exchange of larger missiles with the launching of ICBMs (intercontinental ballistic missiles) that could reach between the United States and the Soviet Union. Thus the IMF treaty, although dealing with only a small percentage of nuclear weapons, nonetheless was seen as an initial and important step toward gradual reduction of nuclear weapons of several broad categories. The following are excerpts of the INF treaty.

γ   γ   γ

* *Department of State Bulletin*, 88 (February 1988), pp. 24–28.

The United States of America and the Union of Soviet Socialist Republics, hereinafter referred to as the Parties,

Conscious that nuclear war would have devastating consequences for all mankind,

Guided by the objective of strengthening strategic stability,

Convinced that the measures set forth in this Treaty will help to reduce the risk of outbreak of war and strengthen internal peace and security, and

Mindful of their obligations under Article VI of the Treaty on the Non-Proliferation of Nuclear Weapons,

Have agreed as follows:

Article 1

In accordance with the provisions of this Treaty which includes the Memorandum of Understanding and Protocols which form an integral part thereof, each party shall eliminate its intermediate-range and shorter-range missiles, not have such systems thereafter, and carry out the other obligations set forth in this Treaty.

Article II

For the purposes of this Treaty:

1. The term "ballistic missile" means a missile that has a ballistic trajectory over most of its flight path. The term "ground-launched ballistic missile (GLBM)" means a ground-launched ballistic missile that is a weapon-delivery system.

2. The term "cruise missile" means an unmanned, self-propelled vehicle that sustains flight through the use of aerodynamic lift over most of its flight path. The term "ground-launched cruise missile (GLCM)" means a ground-launched cruise missile that is a weapon-delivery system.

3. The term "GLBM launcher" means a fixed launcher or a mobile land-based transporter-erector-launcher mechanism for launching a GLBM.

4. The term "GLCM launcher" means a fixed launcher or a mobile land-based transporter-erector-launcher mechanism for launching a GLCM.

5. The term "intermediate-range missile" means a GLBM or a GLCM having a range capability in excess of 1000 kilometers but not in excess of 5500 kilometers.

6. The term "shorter-range missile" means a GLBM or a GLCM having a range capability equal to or in excess of 500 kilometers but not in excess of 1000 kilometers.

7. The term "deployment area" means a designated area within which intermediate-range missiles and launchers of such missiles may operate and within which one or more missile operating bases are located. . . .

10. The term "transit" means movement . . . of an intermediate-range missile or a launcher of such a missile between missile support facilities, between such a facility and a deployment area or between deployment areas, or of a shorter-range missile or a launcher of such a missile from a missile support facility or missile operating base to an elimination facility.

11. The term "deployed missile" means an intermediate-range missile located within a deployment area or a shorter-range missile located at a missile operating base. . . .

13. The term "deployed launcher" means a launcher of an intermediate-range missile located within a deployment area or a launcher of a shorter-range missile located at a missile operating base. . . .

15. The term "basing country" means a country other than the United States of America or the Union of Soviet Socialist Republics on whose territory intermediate-range or shorter-range missiles of the Parties, launchers of such missiles or support structures associated with such missiles and launchers were located at any time after November 1, 1987. Missiles or launchers in transit are not considered to be "located."

Article III

1. For the purposes of this Treaty, existing types of intermediate-range missiles are:

(a) for the United States of America, missiles of the types designated by the United States of American as the Pershing II and the BGM-109G, which are known to the Union of Soviet Socialist Republics by the same designations; and

(b) for the Union of Soviet Socialist Republics, missiles of the types designated by the Union of Soviet Socialist Republics as the RSD-10, the R-12 and the R-14, which are known to the United States of America as the SS-20, the SS-4 and the SS-5, respectively.

2. For the purposes of this Treaty, existing types of shorter-range missiles are:

(a) for the United States of America, missiles of the type designated by the United States of American as the Pershing IA, which is known to the Union of Soviet Socialist Republics by the same designation; and (b) for the Union of Soviet Socialist Republics, missiles of the types designated by the Union of Soviet Socialist Republics as the OTR-22 and the OTR-23, which are known to the United States of America as the SS-12 and the SS-23, respectively.

Article IV

1. Each Party shall eliminate all its intermediate-range missiles and launchers of such missiles, and all support structures and support equipment of the categories listed in the Memorandum of Understanding associated with such missiles and launchers, so that no later than three years after entry into force of this Treaty and thereafter no such missiles, launchers, support structures of support equipment shall be possessed by either Party.

2. To implement paragraph 1 of this Article, upon entry into force of this Treaty, both Parties shall begin and continue throughout the duration of each phase, the reduction of all types of their deployed and non-deployed intermediate-range missiles and deployed and non-deployed launchers of such missiles and support structures and support equipment associated with such missiles and launchers in accordance with the provisions of this Treaty. These reductions shall be implemented in two phases so that:

(a) by the end of the first phase, that is, no later than 29 months after entry into force of this Treaty:

—(i) the number of deployed launchers of intermediate-range missiles for each Party shall not exceed the number of launchers that are capable of carrying or containing at one time missiles considered by the Parties to carry 171 warheads;

—(ii) the number of deployed intermediate-range missiles for each Party shall not exceed the number of such missiles considered by the Parties to carry 180 warheads.

—(iii) the aggregate number of deployed and non-deployed launchers of intermediate-range missiles for each Party shall not exceed the number of launchers that are capable of carrying or containing at one time missiles considered by the Parties to carry 200 warheads;

—(iv) the aggregate number of deployed and non-deployed intermediate-range missiles for each Party shall not exceed the number of such missiles considered by the Parties to carry 200 warheads; and

—(v) the ratio of the aggregate number of deployed and non-deployed intermediate-range GLBMs of existing types for each Party to the aggregate number of deployed and non-deployed intermediate-range missiles of existing types possessed by that Party shall not exceed the ratio of such intermediate-range GLBM's to such intermediate-range missiles for that Party as of November 1, 1987, as set forth in the Memorandum of Understanding; and

(b) by the end of the second phase, that is, no later than three years after entry into force of this Treaty, all intermediate-range missiles of each Party, launchers of such missiles and all support structures and support equipment of the categories listed in the Memorandum of Understanding associated with such missiles and launchers, shall be eliminated.

Article V

1. Each Party shall eliminate all its shorter-range missiles and launchers of such missiles, and all support equipment of the categories listed in the Memorandum of Understanding associated with such missiles and launchers, so that no later than 18 months after entry into force of this Treaty and thereafter no such missiles, launchers or support equipment shall be possessed by either Party.

2. No later than 90 days after entry into force of this Treaty, each Party shall complete the removal of all its deployed shorter-range missiles and deployed and non-deployed launchers of such missiles to elimination facilities and shall retain them at those locations until they are eliminated in accordance with the procedures set forth in the Protocol of Elimination. No later than 12 months after entry into force of this Treaty, each Party shall complete the removal of all its non-deployed shorter-range missiles to elimination facilities and shall retain them at those locations until they are eliminated in accordance with the procedures set forth in the Protocol on Elimination.

3. Shorter-range missiles and launchers of such missiles shall not be located at the same elimination facility. Such facilities shall be separated by no less than 1000 kilometers.

Article VI

1. Upon entry into force of this Treaty and thereafter, neither Party shall:

(a) produce or flight-test any intermediate-range missiles or produce any stages of such missiles or any launchers of such missiles; or

(b) produce, flight-test or launch any shorter-range missiles or produce any stages of such missiles or any launchers of such missiles. . . .

Article IX

1. For the purpose of ensuring verification of compliance with the provisions of this Treaty, each Party shall have the right to conduct on-site inspections. The Parties shall implement on-site inspections in accordance with this Article, the Protocol on Inspection and the Protocol on Elimination. . . .

DOCUMENT 37

ANTI-GORBACHEV RESOLUTION, 1990*

Mikhail Gorbachev's attempts to implement substantial political and economic reforms in the Soviet Union, after he came to power in 1985, created uncertainty and even opposition among segments of the Soviet population. His concept of "perestroika" (restructuring or reforming) questioned established practices followed for many decades since the days of Lenin and Stalin. In addition, reacting to Gorbachev's powerful role as the General Secretary of the Communist Party, many middle- and high-level communists saw him as a threat to their positions and authority. By 1988–89, the Communist Party increasingly was divided into pro- and anti-Gorbachev factions over the perestroika issue. In 1990 a group of party conservatives passed the following resolution of no-confidence in Gorbachev and demanded his dismissal.

γ   γ   γ

To the TSK KPSS [Central Committee of the Communist Party of the Soviet Union]
RESOLUTION of the 3rd All-Union Conference of the Society "Unity, For Leninism and Communist Ideals"—October 28, 1990, Leningrad

ON THE LACK OF CONFIDENCE IN THE POLICIES OF THE GENERAL SECRETARY OF THE CENTRAL COMMITTEE OF THE COMMUNIST PARTY OF THE SOVIET UNION [CC CPSU] M. S. GORBACHEV.

* http://www.ibiblio.org/expo/soviet.exhibit/ab2unity.html.

Faced with catastrophic consequences for the people, the country, and the party due to M. S. Gorbachev's policy of so-called "Perestroika", and in view of the fact that this policy has absolutely revealed its bourgeois-restorationist character, and in consideration of the fact that we are on the brink of an even greater national catastrophe in connection with the planned implementation in the country of the "stabilization program" from the International Monetary Fund, which is disguised as a transition program toward a market economy, the 3rd All-Union Conference of the Society "Unity, for Leninism and Communist Ideals," expresses its lack of confidence in the policies of M. S. Gorbachev as General Secretary of the CC CPSU.

We feel that the only force in the country capable of changing the course of the events in a constructive way, without leading to civil war, to date continues to remain the Communist Party.

We invite all honest, socialistically- and patriotically-oriented members of the CPSU, members of the Central Committee and the CC CPSU, party organizations at all levels, and the communist parties of all union republics to request the convening of a special meeting of the CPSU, to raise the question of:
1. The dismissal of M. S. Gorbachev and his more zealous associates, who were involved in the unleashing of a bourgeois counterrevolution in the Soviet Union, from all elected party posts and about their exclusion from the ranks of the Communist Party of the Soviet Union.
2. The recall of M. S. Gorbachev and said persons from deputy posts, to which they were appointed only because they were party functionaries.
3. The immediate removal of the country from this general national crisis not along the path of the restoration of capitalism but of socialist renewal.
4. An investigation into the real reasons and processes that formed this crisis situation during 1985–1990, which is unprecedented in terms of severity and danger for the Soviet government, and calling the guilty to account before the party and the country.

The All-Union Society "UNITY" recommends that all members of the organization develop propaganda campaigns for this resolution at the local level, firstly, by means of conducting open party, trade-union and similar meetings, to achieve the concurrence of CPSU party organizations.

Forward the proceeding from the open All-Union Party Conference to call M. S. Gorbachev to account before the Party to the CC CPSU, to newspapers, and to the political executive committee of "Unity." The resolution was accepted unanimously.

Chairman of the political executive committee of the All-Union Society "Unity—for Leninism and Communist Ideals." [signed] N. Andreeva

DOCUMENT 38

THE CONVENTIONAL ARMED FORCES TREATY, 1990*

The two contending military alliance systems in Europe during the Cold War era, the North Atlantic Treaty Organization (NATO) and the Warsaw Pact, began negotiations in the late 1980s to reduce military weaponry and thus lessen tensions in the European region. The end of communist regimes in East Europe in 1989 helped resolve some strategic issues in the region. A prominent example of this effort is the Conventional Armed Forces in Europe Treaty (CFE), signed November 19, 1990 by twenty-two governments in NATO and the Warsaw Pact: Belgium, Bulgaria, Canada, Czech Republic, Denmark, France, Germany, Greece, Hungary, Iceland, Italy, Luxembourg, Netherlands, Norway, Poland, Portugal, Romania, Spain, Turkey, Union of Soviet Socialist Republics, United Kingdom, and United States. The treaty made extensive cuts in weapons systems on both sides, as well as creating verification procedures to monitor these reductions. By 1991 the Warsaw Pact ended and later that year the Soviet Union broke up into fifteen separate states with the collapse of the communist nation. The governments in the CFE agreement met periodically during the decade of the 1990s to promote full implementation of the treaty. The following are portions of this lengthy, detailed, and complex agreement.

γ   γ   γ

* http://dosfan.lib.uic.edu/acda/treaties/cfe.htm.

Article 1

1. Each State Party shall carry out the obligations set forth in this Treaty in accordance with its provisions, including those obligations relating to the following five categories of conventional armed forces: battle tanks, armoured combat vehicles, artillery, combat aircraft and combat helicopters.

2. Each State Party also shall carry out the other measures set forth in this Treaty designed to ensure security and stability both during the period of reduction of conventional armed forces and after the completion of reductions. . . .

Article IV

1. Within the area of application . . . each State Party shall limit and, as necessary, reduce its battle tanks, armoured combat vehicles, artillery, combat aircraft and attack helicopters so that, 40 months after entry into force of the Treaty and thereafter, for the group of States Parties to which it belongs . . . the aggregate numbers do not exceed:

(A) 20,000 battle tanks, of which no more than 16,500 shall be in active units;

(B) 30,000 armoured combat vehicles, of which no more than 27,300 shall be in active units. Of the 30,000 armoured combat vehicles, no more than 18,000 shall be armoured infantry fighting vehicles and heavy armament combat vehicles; of armoured infantry fighting vehicles and heavy armament combat vehicles, no more than 1,500 shall be heavy armament combat vehicles;

(C) 20,000 pieces of artillery, of which no more than 17,000 shall be in active units;

(D) 6,800 combat aircraft; and

(E) 2,000 attack helicopters.

Battle tanks, armoured combat vehicles and artillery not in active units shall be placed in designated permanent storage sites. . . .

2. Within the area consisting of the entire land territory in Europe . . . each State Party shall limit and, as necessary, reduce its battle tanks, armoured combat vehicles and artillery so that, 40 months after entry into force of this Treaty and thereafter, for the group of States Parties to which it belong the aggregate numbers do not exceed:

(A) 15,300 battle tanks, of which no more than 11,800 shall be in active units;

(B) 24,000 armoured combat vehicles, of which no more than 21,400 shall be in active units; and

(C) 14,000 pieces of artillery, of which no more than 11,000 shall be in active units. . . .

Article VI

With the objective of ensuring that no single State Party possesses more than approximately one-third of the conventional armaments and equipment limited by the Treaty within the area of application, each State Party shall limit and, as necessary, reduce its battle tanks, armoured combat vehicles, artillery, combat aircraft and attack helicopters so that, 40 months after entry into force of this Treaty and thereafter, the numbers within the area of application for that State Party do not exceed:

(A) 13,300 battle tanks;

(B) 20,000 armoured combat vehicles;

(C) 13,700 pieces of artillery;

(D) 5,150 combat aircraft. . . .

Article VII

1. In order that the limitations set forth in Articles IV, V and VI are not exceeded, no State Party shall exceed, from 40 months after entry into force of this Treaty, the maximum levels which it has previously agreed upon within its group of States Parties . . . for its holding of conventional armament and equipment limited by the Treaty and of which it has provided notification pursuant to the provisions of this Article.

2. Each State Party shall provide at the signature of this Treaty notification to all other States Parties of the maximum levels for its holding of conventional armament and equipment limited by the Treaty. The notification of the maximum levels for holdings of conventional armaments and equipment limited by the Treaty provided by each State Party at the signature of this Treaty shall remain valid until the date specified in a subsequent notification. . . .

3. In accordance with the limitations set forth in Articles IV, V and VI, each State Party shall have the right to change the maximum levels for its holdings of conventional armaments and equipment limited by the

Treaty. Any change in the maximum levels for holdings of a State Party shall be notified by that State Party to all other States Parties at least 90 days in advance of the date, specific in the notification, on which such a change takes effect. In order not to exceed any of the limitations set forth in Articles IV and V, any increase in the maximum levels for holdings of a State Party that would otherwise cause those limitations to be exceeded shall be preceded or accompanied by a corresponding reduction in the previously notified maximum levels for holding of conventional armaments and equipment limited by the Treaty of one or more States Parties belonging to the same group of States Parties. . . .

Article VIII. . . .

2. The categories of conventional armament and equipment subject to reductions are battle tanks, armoured combat vehicles, artillery, combat aircraft and attack helicopters. The specific types are listed in the Protocol on Existing Types.

(A) Battle tanks and armoured combat vehicles shall be reduced by destruction, conversion for non-military purposes, placement on static display, [or] use as ground targets. . . .

(B) Artillery shall be reduced by destruction or placement on static display, or, in the case of self-propelled artillery, by use as ground targets.

(C) Combat aircraft shall be reduced by destruction, placement on static display, use for ground instructional purposes, or, in the case of specific models or versions of combat-capable trainer aircraft, reclassification into unarmed trainer aircraft.

(D) Specialized attack helicopters shall be reduced by destruction, placement on static display, or use for ground instructional purposes.

(E) Multi-purpose attack helicopters shall be reduced by destruction, placement on static display, use for ground instructional purposes, or recategorization. . . .

4. Reductions shall be effected in three phases and completed no later than 40 months after entry into force of this Treaty, so that:

(A) by the end of the first reduction phase, that is, no later than 16 months after entry into force of this Treaty, each State Party shall have ensured that at least 25 percent of its total reduction liability in each of the categories of conventional armaments and equipment limited by the Treaty has been reduced;

(B) by the end of the second reduction phase, that is, no later than 28 months after entry into force of this Treaty, each State Party shall have ensured that at least 60 percent of its total reduction liability in each of the categories of conventional armaments and equipment limited by the Treaty has been reduced;

(C) by the end of the third reduction phase, that is, no later than 40 months after entry into force of this Treaty, each State Party shall have reduced its total reduction liability in each of the categories of conventional armaments and equipment limited by the Treaty. . . .

Article XIII

1. For the purpose of ensuring verification of compliance with the provisions of this Treaty, each State Party shall provide notifications and exchange information pertaining to its conventional armaments and equipment in accordance with the Protocol on Information Exchange. . . .

Article XIV

1. For the purpose of ensuring verification of compliance with the provisions of this Treaty, each State Party shall have the right to conduct, and the obligation to accept, within the areas of application, inspections in accordance with the provisions of the Protocol of Inspection.

2. The purpose of such inspections shall be:

(A) to verify, on the basis of the information provided pursuant to the Protocol on Information Exchange, the compliance of States Parties with the numerical limitations set forth in Article IV, V and VI;

(B) to monitor the process of reduction of battle tanks, armoured combat vehicles, artillery, combat aircraft and attack helicopters carried out at reduction sites . . . ; and

(C) to monitor the certification of recategorized multi-purpose attack helicopters and reclassified combat-capable trainer aircraft carried out in accordance with the Protocol on Helicopter Recategorization and the Protocol on Aircraft Reclassification, respectively. . . .

Article XVIII

1. The States Parties, after signature of this Treaty, shall continue the negotiations on conventional armed forces with the same Mandate and with the goal of building on this Treaty.

2. The objective for these negotiations shall be to conclude an agree-

ment on additional measures aimed at further strengthening security and stability in Europe, and pursuant to the Mandate, including measures to limit the personnel strength of their conventional armed forces within the area of application.

3. The States Parties shall seek to conclude these negotiations no later than the follow-up meeting of the Conference on Security and Cooperation in Europe to be held in Helsinki in 1992.

Article XIX

1. This Treaty shall be of unlimited duration. It may be supplemented by a further treaty.

2. Each State Party shall, in exercising its national sovereignty, have the right to withdraw from this Treaty if it decides that extraordinary events related to the subject matter of this Treaty have jeopardized its supreme interests. A State Party intending to withdraw shall give notice of its decision to do so to the Depositary and to all other States Parties. Such notice shall be given at least 150 days prior to the intended withdrawal from this Treaty. It shall include a statement of the extraordinary events the State Party regards as having jeopardized its supreme interests.

3. Each State Party shall, in particular, in exercising its national sovereignty, have the right to withdraw from this Treaty if another State Party increases its holdings in battle tanks, armoured combat vehicles, artillery, combat aircraft or attack helicopters . . . which are outside the scope of the limitations of this Treaty, in such proportions as to pose an obvious threat to the balance of forces within the area of application.

. . .

DOCUMENT 39

GORBACHEV DEFENDS PERESTROIKA, 1991*

Mikhail Gorbachev became the Secretary General of the Communist Party of the Soviet Union (CPSU) in March 1985, and identified numerous problems facing his nation: the lethargic Soviet economy, mounting social tensions across the nation, and growing disillusionment with the Com-

---

* By permission of the Norwegian Nobel Institute.

*munist Party. Gorbachev called for "glasnost" ("openness") to publicly rec-
ognize the existence of these problems in order to seek solutions. This encouraged widespread comment in the media and public opinion. He also began
substantial modifications in foreign policy, resulting in better relations with
the West, and for which he was awarded the Nobel Peace Prize in 1990. His
reform efforts in domestic policies and foreign affairs from 1985 until he fell
from power in 1991 are known as "perestroika" (usually translated as "restructuring"). The following excerpts, from a speech Gorbachev gave in June
1991 upon receiving the Nobel Peace Prize, describe "perestroika." By that
time, he had the perspective of sufficient time to assess the mixed results of
his attempted reforms. A few months later, Gorbachev was forced to resign
and in December 1991 the Soviet Union disintegrated into fifteen independent nations.*

γ   γ   γ

I see the decision to award me the Nobel Peace Prize . . . as an act of
solidarity with the monumental undertaking which has already placed
enormous demands on the Soviet people in terms of efforts, costs, hard-
ships, willpower, and character. And solidarity is a universal value which
is becoming indispensable for progress and for the survival of human-
kind. But a modern state has to be worthy of solidarity, in other words,
it should pursue, in both domestic and international affairs, policies that
bring together the interests of the people and those of the world community. This task, however obvious, is not a simple one. Life is much
richer and more complex than even the most perfect plans to make it
better. It ultimately takes vengeance for attempts to impose abstract
schemes, even with the best of intentions. Perestroika has made us understand this about our past, and the actual experience of recent years
has taught us to reckon with the most general laws of civilization.

This, however, came later. But back in March–April 1985 we found ourselves facing a crucial, and I confess, agonizing choice. When I agreed
to assume the office of the General Secretary of the CPSU Central
Committee, in effect the highest State office at that time, I realized that
we could not longer live as before and that I would not want to remain
in that office unless I got support in undertaking major reforms. It was
clear to me that we had a long way to go. But of course, I did not imagine how immense were our problems and difficulties. I believe no one at
that time could foresee or predict them.

Those who then were governing the country knew what was really happening to it and what we later called "zastoi," roughly translated as stagnation. They saw that our society was marking time, that it was running the risk of falling hopelessly behind the technologically advanced part of the world. Total domination of centrally-managed state property, the pervasive authoritarian-bureaucratic system, ideology's grip on politics, monopoly in social thought and sciences, militarized industries that siphoned off our best, including the best intellectual resources, the unbearable burden of military expenditures that suffocated civilian industries and undermined the social achievements of the period since the [1917] Revolution which were real and of which we used to be proud—such was the actual situation in the country.

As a result, one of the richest countries in the world, endowed with immense overall potential, was already sliding downwards. Our society was declining, both economically and intellectually. And yet, to a casual observer the country seemed to present a picture of relative well-being, stability and order. The misinformed society under the spell of propaganda was hardly aware of what was going on and what the immediate future kept in store for it. The slightest manifestations of protest were suppressed. Most people considered them heretical, slanderous and counter-revolutionary.

Such was the situation in the spring of 1985, and there was a great temptation to leave things as they were, to make only cosmetic changes. This, however, meant continuing to deceive ourselves and the people. This was the domestic aspect of the dilemma then before us. As for the foreign policy aspect, there was the East-West confrontation, a rigid division into friends and foes, the two hostile camps with a corresponding set of Cold War attributes. Both the East and the West were constrained by the logic of military confrontation, wearing themselves down more and more by the arms race. The mere thought of dismantling the existing structures did not come easily. However, the realization that we faced inevitable disaster, both domestically and internationally, gave us the strength to make a historic choice, which I have never since regretted.

Perestroika, which once again is returning our people to common sense, has enabled us to open up to the world and has restored a normal relationship between the country's internal development and its foreign policy. But all this takes a lot of hard work. To a people which believed that its government's policies had always been true to the cause of peace, we proposed what was in many ways a different policy, which would genuinely serve the cause of peace, while differing from the prevailing view of what it meant and particularly from the established stereotypes as to how one should protect it. We proposed new thinking in foreign policy. Thus we embarked on a path of many changes, which may turn out to be the most significant in the twentieth century, for our country and for its peoples. But we also did it for the entire world.

I began my [1987] book about perestroika and the new thinking with the following words: "We want to be understood." After a while I felt that it was already happening. But now I would like once again to repeat those words here, from this world rostrum. Because to understand us really—to understand so as to believe us—proved to be not at all easy, owing to the immensity of the changes under way in our country. . . . Applying conventional wisdom to perestroika is unproductive. It is also futile and dangerous to set conditions to say: We'll understand and believe you, as soon as you, the Soviet Union, come completely to resemble "us", the West.

No one is in a position to describe in detail what perestroika will finally produce. But it would certainly be a self-delusion to expect that perestroika will produce "a copy" of anything. Of course, learning from the experience of others is something we have been doing and will continue to do. But this does not mean that we will come to be exactly like others. Our State will preserve its own identity with the international community. A country like ours, with its uniquely close-knit ethnic composition, cultural diversity and tragic past, the greatness of its historic endeavors and the exploits of its peoples—such a country will find its own path to the civilization of the twenty-first century and its own place in it. Perestroika has to be conceived solely in this context, otherwise it will fail and will be rejected. After all, it is impossible to "shed" the country's thousand-year history—a history, which we still have to subject to serious analysis in order to find the truth that we shall take to the future. . . .

A period of transition to a new quality in all spheres of society's life is accompanied by painful phenomena. When we were initiating perestroika we failed to properly assess and foresee everything. Our society turned out to be hard to move off the ground, not ready for major changes which affect people's vital interests and make them leave behind everything to which they had become accustomed over many years. In the beginning we imprudently generated great expectations, without taking into account the fact that it takes time for people to realize that all have to live and work differently, to stop expecting that new life would be given from above.

Perestroika has now entered its most dramatic phase. Following the transformation of the philosophy of perestroika into real policy, which began literally to explode the old way of life, difficulties began to mount. Many took fright and wanted to return to the past. It was not only those who used to hold the levers of power in the administration, the army and various government agencies and who had to make room, but also many people whose interests and way of life was put to a severe test and who, during the preceding decades, had forgotten how to take the initiative and to be independent, enterprising and self-reliant.

Hence the discontent, the outbursts of protest and the exorbitant, though understandable, demands which, if satisfied right away, would lead to complete chaos. Hence the rising political passions and, instead of a constructive opposition, which is only normal in a modern democratic system, one that is often destructive and unreasonable, not to mention the extremist forces, which are especially cruel and inhuman in areas of inter-ethnic conflict.

During the last six years we have discarded and destroyed much that stood in the way of a renewal and transformation of our society. But when society was given freedom it could not recognize itself, for it had lived too long, as it were, "beyond the looking glass". Contradictions and vices rose to the surface, and even blood has been shed, although we have been able to avoid a bloodbath. The logic of reform has clashed with the logic of their rejection, and with the logic of impatience which breeds intolerance.

In this situation, which is one of great opportunity and of major risks, at a high point of perestroika's crisis, our task is to stay the course while also addressing current everyday problems—which are literally tearing this policy apart—and to do it in such a way as to prevent a social and political explosion. Now about my position. As to the fundamental choice I have long ago made a final and irrevocable decision. Nothing and no one, no pressure, either from the right or from the left, will make me abandon the positions of perestroika and new thinking. I do not intend to change my views or convictions. My choice is a final one. . . .

DOCUMENT 40

THE MAASTRICHT TREATY, 1992*

A major step forward in the integration efforts of the members of the European Community occurred in December 1991 when their negotiations at Maastricht, Netherlands, formulated a comprehensive plan that brought them closer to their objectives to link their political, economic, monetary, social, legal, and defense systems. It included extensive procedures to develop and implement a common foreign policy. The decision to adopt a common currency (the "euro") also emerged from this meeting. The governments signed the treaty, titled the "Treaty on European Union," on February 7, 1992. The timetable for these states, now designated the European Union (EU), laid out the steps for greater integration by the end of the decade and continuing into the early 21st century. The earlier sections of this lengthy agreement are given below.

γ   γ   γ

[The governments of Belgium, Denmark, France, Germany, Greece, Ireland, Italy, Luxembourg, Netherlands, Portugal, Spain, and the United Kingdom],

Resolved to mark a new stage in the process of European integration undertaken with the establishment of the European Communities,

Recalling the historic importance of the ending of the division of the European continent and the need to create firm bases for the construction of the future Europe,

Confirming their attachment to the principles of liberty, democracy and respect for human rights and fundamental freedoms and of the rule of law,

Confirming their attachment to fundamental social rights as defined in the European Social Charter signed at Turin [Italy] on 18 October 1962

* http://europe.eu.int/eur-lex/en/treaties/dat/eu_cons_treaty_en.pdf.

and in the 1989 Community Charter of the Fundamental Social Rights of Workers,

Desiring to deepen the solidarity between their peoples while respecting their history, their culture and their traditions,

Desiring to enhance further the democratic and efficient functioning of the institutions so as to enable them better to carry out, within a single institutional framework, the tasks entrusted to them,

Resolved to achieve the strengthening and the convergence of their economies and to establish an economic and monetary union including, in accordance with the provisions of this Treaty, a single and stable currency,

Determined to promote economic and social progress for their peoples, taking into account the principle of sustainable development and within the context of the accomplishments of the internal market and of reinforced cohesion and environmental protection, and to implement policies ensuring that advances in economic integration are accompanied by parallel progress in other fields,

Resolved to establish a citizenship common to nationals of their countries,

Resolved to implement a common foreign and security policy including the progressive framing of a common defence policy, which might lead to a common defence in accordance with the provisions of Article 17, thereby reinforcing the European identity and its independence in order to promote peace, security and progress in Europe and in the world,

Resolved to facilitate the free movement of persons, while ensuring the safety and security of their peoples, by establishing an area of freedom, security and justice, in accordance with the provisions of this Treaty,

Resolved to continue the process of creating an ever closer union among the peoples of Europe, in which decisions are taken as closely as possible to the citizen in accordance with the principle of subsidiarity,

In view of further steps to be taken in order to advance European integration,

Have decided to establish a European Union . . .

Article 1

By this Treaty, the High Contracting Parties establish among themselves a European Union, hereinafter called 'the Union'. This Treaty marks a new stage in the process of creating an ever closer union among the peoples of Europe, in which decisions are taken as openly as possible and as closely as possible to the citizen. . . .

Article 2

The Union shall set itself the following objectives:

[a] to promote economic and social progress and a high level of employment and to achieve balanced and sustainable development, in particular through the creation of an area without internal frontiers, through the strengthening of economic and social cohesion and through the establishment of economic and monetary union, ultimately including a single currency in accordance with the provisions of this Treaty;

[b] to assert its identity on the international scene, in particular through the implementation of a common foreign and security policy including the progressive framing of a common defence policy, which might lead to a common defence, in accordance with the provisions of Article 17;

[c] to strengthen the protection of the rights and interests of the nationals of its Member States through the introduction of a citizenship of the Union;

[d] to maintain and develop the Union as an area of freedom, security and justice, in which the free movement of persons is assured in conjunction with appropriate measures with respect to external border controls, asylum, immigration and the prevention and combatting of crime;

[e] to maintain in full the acquis communautaire [sic] and build on it with a view to considering to what extent the policies and forms of cooperation introduced by this Treaty may need to be revised with the aim of ensuring the effectiveness of the mechanisms and the institutions of the Community.

The objectives of the Union shall be achieved as provided in the Treaty and in accordance with the conditions and the timetable set out therein while respecting the principle of subsidiarity as defined in Article 5 of the Treaty establishing the European Community.

Article 3

The Union shall be served by a single institutional framework which shall ensure the consistency and the continuity of the activities carried out in order to attain its objectives while respecting and building upon the acquis communautaire [sic]. . . .

Article 4

The European Council shall provide the Union with the necessary impetus for its development and shall define the general political guidelines thereof. The European Council shall bring together the Heads of

State or Government of the Member States and the President of the Commission. They shall be assisted by the Ministers for Foreign Affairs of the Member States and by a Member of the Commission. The European Council shall meet at least twice a year, under the chairmanship of the Head of State or Government of the Member State which holds the Presidency of the Council. The European Council shall submit to the European Parliament a report after each of its meetings and a yearly written report on the progress achieved by the Union. . . .

Article 6

1. The Union is founded on the principles of liberty, democracy, respect for human rights and fundamental freedoms, and the rule of law, principles which are common to the Member States.
2. The Union shall respect fundamental rights . . . as general principles of Community law.
3. The Union shall respect the national identities of its Member States.
4. The Union shall provide itself with the means necessary to attain its objectives and carry through its policies.

Article 7

1. The Council, meeting in the composition of the Heads of State or Government and acting by unanimity on a proposal by one third of the Member States or by the Commission and after obtaining the assent of the European Parliament, may determine the existence of a serious and persistent breach by a Member State of principles mentioned in Article 6(1), after inviting the government of the Member State in question to submit its observations.
2. Where such a determination has been made, the Council, acting by a qualified majority, may decide to suspend certain of the rights deriving from the application of the Treaty to the Member State in question, including the voting rights of the representative of the government of that Member State in the Council. In doing so, the Council shall take into account the possible consequences of such a suspension on the right and obligations of natural and legal persons. The obligations of the Member State in question under this Treaty shall in any case continue to be binding on that State.
3. The Council, acting by a qualified majority, may decide subsequently to vary or revoke measures taken under paragraph 2 in response to change in the situation which led to their being imposed. . . .
5. For the purposes of this Article, The European Parliament shall act

by a two-thirds majority of the votes cast, representing a majority of its members. . . .

Article 11

1. The Union shall define and implement a common foreign and security policy covering all areas of foreign and security policy, the objectives of which shall be:

[a] to safeguard the common values, fundamental interests, independence and integrity of the Union in conformity with the principles of the United Nations Charter;

[b] to strengthen the security of the Union in all ways;

[c] to preserve peace and strengthen international security, in accordance with the principles of the United Nations Charter, as well as the principles of the Helsinki Final Act and the objectives of the Paris Charter, including those on external borders;

[d] to promote international cooperation;

[e] to develop and consolidate democracy and the rule of law, and respect for human rights and fundamental freedoms.

2. The Member States shall support the Union's external and security policy actively and unreservedly in a spirit of loyalty and mutual solidarity. The Member States shall work together to enhance and develop their mutual political solidarity. They shall refrain from any action which is contrary to the interests of the Union or likely to impair its effectiveness as a cohesive force in international relations. The Council shall ensure that these principles are complied with. . . .

Article 13

1. The European Council shall define the principles of and general guidelines for the common foreign and security policy, including for matters with defence implications.

2. The European Council shall decide on common strategies to be implemented by the Union in areas where the Member States have important interests in common.

Article 14

1. The Council shall adopt joint actions. Joint actions shall address specific situations where operational action by the Union is deemed to be required. They shall lay down their objectives, scope, the means to be made available to the Union, if necessary their duration, and the conditions for their implementation. . . .

Article 17

1. The common foreign and security policy shall include all questions relating to the security of the Union, including the progressive framing of a common defence policy, in accordance with the second subparagraph, which might lead to a common defence, should the European Council so decide. It shall in that case recommend to the Member States the adoption of such a decision in accordance with their respective constitutional requirement. . . .

The policy of the Union in accordance with this article shall not prejudice the specific character of the security and defence policy of certain Member States and shall respect the obligations of certain Member States, which see their common defence realised in the North Atlantic Treaty Organization (NATO) under the North Atlantic Treaty, and be compatible with the common security and defence policy established within that framework. The progressive framing of a common defence policy will be supported, as Member States consider appropriate, by co-operation between them in the field of armaments.

2. Questions referred to in this Article shall include humanitarian and rescue tasks, peacekeeping tasks and tasks of combat forces in crisis management, including peacekeeping. . . .

Article 49

Any European State which respects the principles set out in Article 6(1) may apply to become a member of the Union. It shall address its application to the Council, which shall act unanimously after consulting the Commission and after receiving the assent of the European Parliament, which shall act by an absolute majority of its component members. The conditions of admission and the adjustments to the Treaties on which the Union is founded which such admission entails shall be the subject of an agreement between the Member States and the applicant State. This agreement shall be submitted for ratification by all the contracting States in accordance with their respective constitutional requirements. . . .

Article 51

This Treaty is concluded for an unlimited period. . . .

Article 52

1. This Treaty shall be ratified by the High Contracting Parties in accordance with their respective constitutional requirements. The instru-

ment of ratification shall be deposited with the Government of the Italian Republic.

2. This Treaty shall enter into force on 1 January 1993, provided that all the instruments of ratification have been deposited, or, failing that, on the first day of the month following the deposit of the instrument of ratification by the last signatory State to take this step. . . .

DOCUMENT 41

THE PARTNERSHIP FOR PEACE, 1994*

The collapse of communist regimes in East Europe in 1989–1990 and the breakup of the Soviet Union in 1991 created opportunities for greater European stability in the post-communist era. Although the Warsaw Pact composed of the Soviet Union and its allies no longer existed, the North Atlantic Treaty Organization (NATO) still remained. Extensive discussions within NATO assessed whether it also should disband. Out of these consultations emerged the "Partnership for Peace" when non-NATO states, especially those of the former Warsaw Pact, were invited to participate in a cooperative association with the Western alliance and further reduce the tensions of the Cold War. The plan did not guarantee that those "partners" would join NATO, but the possibility existed in the long term. Many states joined the Partnership for Peace, including Russia, Ukraine, and East European nations. The following is a 1994 statement explaining this arrangement by Gebhardt von Moltke, NATO's Assistant Secretary General for Political Affairs.

γ   γ   γ

Partnership for Peace, launched at the NATO Summit in Brussels last January [1994], is a new and ambitious initiative intended to enhance stability and security in the whole of Europe by strengthening the relationship between NATO and the countries of Central and Eastern Europe and other CSCE [Conference on Security and Cooperation in Europe] participating states.

In effect, Partnership for Peace is an invitation to these countries to deepen and intensify their ties with the Alliance through practical co-

* By permission of *NATO Review*, 42 (June 1994), pp. 3–7.

operation. Much of this will be in the military sphere, and will concentrate on fostering the stability to work together in such fields as peacekeeping and humanitarian assistance. In addition, the Partnership has a wider, more political dimension to it, which is is the promotion of, and commitment to, democratic principles, thereby increasing stability and diminishing threats to peace.

There has been remarkable progress in implementing Partnership for Peace since its launch. Within 10 weeks of the Summit, seven NATO briefing teams had visited 16 different countries and the CSCE Secretariat in Vienna in response to requests for further information. These visits were headed at ambassadorial level and they allowed for a very detailed provision of information and exchanges of views on the implementation of Partnership for Peace.

The speed at which partners have responded to the invitation gives some indication of the importance attached to the initiative. Twenty countries had joined by 1 June, including Finland and Sweden. Others, and among those, Russia, have indicated their intention of doing so.

The Partnership for Peace (PFP) builds on several years of continually increasing dialogue and cooperation under the North Atlantic Cooperation Council (NACC). The NACC, formed in December 1991, is composed of the 16 NATO nations and the countries of Central and Eastern Europe and others which gained independence following the dissolution of the Soviet Union. For their part, Allied leaders committed themselves to support reform in the new and independent states of Central and Eastern Europe; to give practical assistance to them; and to build confidence through increased contacts.

The result was a process of dialogue, partnership and cooperation that gained tangible expression through the implementation of an annual NACC Work Plan. This Work Plan has concentrated on raising the general level of cooperation and understanding between NATO and its partners through a broad and diverse range of cooperation activities, including consultations on security-related matters and extensive military contacts.

Partnership for Peace was thus launched at a time when cooperation was a well-established reality rather than an aspiration. But PFP differs significantly in intensity and scope from what has gone before. It goes beyond and enhances the dialogue and cooperation undertaken through the NACC process and moves from general common activities to individual, tailored programmes of cooperation between NATO and each of its partners. The wider scope of PFP is reflected in its objectives, as set out in the Framework Document, issued at the Brussels Summit, i.e.:

1. to facilitate transparency in national defence planning and budgeting processes;

2. to ensure democratic control of defence forces;

3. to maintain the capability and readiness to contribute, subject to constitutional considerations, to operations under the authority of the UN and/or the responsibility of the CSCE;

4. to develop cooperative military relations with NATO, for the purpose of joint planning, training, and exercises in order to strengthen their ability to undertake missions in the fields of peacekeeping, search and rescue, humanitarian operations, and others as may subsequently be agreed; and

5. to develop, over the longer term, forces that are better able to operate with those of the members of the North Atlantic Alliance.

The achievement of these objectives will contribute practically to the security and stability of Europe by building on the foundations laid down by the NACC. Partnership for Peace therefore remains within the overall framework of the NACC. However, the experience, interests and capacities of NATO's partners vary significantly and thus the pace and scope of cooperation under the PFP will reflect the requirements of each individual partner.

The Partnership is, and will remain, an equal opportunity for all, while allowing each partner to develop progressively closer relations with the Alliance on the basis of its own interest and actual performance. This is not a kind of competition or race, however. It simply reflects the reality that countries develop in different ways and at varying rates. The range of cooperative possibilities and interests with a country as large as Russia, for example, is likely to be greater than that with smaller countries, hence, the need to tailor cooperation programmes to each particular partner.

The Partnership is far-reaching in its ambition to establish the kind of understanding and habits of cooperation with partners that have long existed among Allies. While it may take some partners longer than others to achieve this, the opportunity of doing so is open to all.

The PFP invitation is addressed to every state participating in the NACC as well as other CSCE countries able and willing to contribute to this programme. Slovenia became the first non-NACC country to join the Partnership at the end of March [1994], and Finland and Sweden did so at the beginning of May. Participation by such countries extends the Alliance's efforts into new areas, underlining the point that PFP is not simply about reducing divisions and misunderstandings between old adversaries but has a new agenda, looking forward, rather than back.

Under PFP, activities and contacts are set to increase significantly. To date, partner countries have sent representatives to NACC meetings and activities, either from their capitals or from their embassies in Brussels. This has worked well in the past, but as the intensity of our work increases, then so will the need for frequent, even daily contact. The Brussels Summit therefore invited PFP partners to establish their own liaison offices at NATO Headquarters in Brussels to facilitate their participation in NACC/PFP meetings and activities. Except for a few with well-established diplomatic missions in Brussels, all the partner countries which have joined the PFP have indicated their desire to take up NATO's offer of permanent facilities at NATO Headquarters, facilities which have already been constructed.

Another feature of the PFP is the establishment of a Partnership Coordination Cell at Mons, Belgium, where Supreme Headquarters, Allied Powers Europe (SHAPE) is also located. It will carry out, under the authority of the NATO Council, the military coordination and planning necessary to implement PFP programmes. PFP partners have been invited to send permanent liaison officers to the Coordination Cell and most of them are preparing officers for this assignment. Office facilities have been made available at Mons and the Coordination Cell will begin shortly.

One of the main focuses of Partnership for Peace is the development of greater cooperation in the field of peacekeeping. NATO and partner countries are increasingly likely to find themselves side-by-side in re-sponding to, and implementing, UN and CSCE mandates. The need for more coherent preparation for peacekeeping missions has grown more urgent as a result of the increased risks and greater demands for military forces for such operations as those in former Yugoslavia. Our military forces have to learn not only to work together, but also to support and rely on each other.

Useful progress has already been made in the NACC Ad Hoc Group on Peacekeeping where various aspects of multinational peacekeeping operations have been addressed, including the need for training and exercise as a means to promote common approaches and understanding of this task. The value of this work has been recognized by the UN, CSCE and by such non-NACC states as Austria, Finland and Sweden, who have all sent observers or participated in the Ad Hoc Group's work, which will now be carried forward and augmented through PFP.

Field exercises, to promote closer peacekeeping cooperation and interoperability, will be a major aspect of Partnership for Peace. The planning for three exercises, two land and the other maritime, is now well under way and it has been decided that the first will take place in the Netherlands in October. These are intended to exercise and simulate common peacekeeping tasks so as to improve the ability of partners to work together in actual missions. Partners will not only be fully involved in the planning, they may also host an exercise on their territory. Poland, for example, will be the first partner country to host a peacekeeping field exercise this coming autumn.

The concept of interoperability in peacekeeping is aimed at ensuring compatibility in approaches and procedures, not at common or standardized equipment. Exercises, for example, will seek to improve communications and operating procedures among participants. Since peacekeeping is a field of activity where both allies and partners have experience to offer and share, cooperation in this field is breaking new ground. This is genuinely a two-way street.

Partnership for Peace is more however than a programme of activities. It also aims at developing closer political ties. In launching the Partnership, NATO's leaders thus gave a commitment to consult with any active participant if the partner perceives a direct threat to its territorial integrity, political independence, or security. This offers a channel for consultation with the Alliance on possible future crises and on ways in which they might be defused. . . .

The concrete achievements over the past several months in establishing the substance, modalities and structures of Partnership for Peace show that the momentum of the Brussels Summit is being translated into action. A significant aspect of PFP is its potential for further development and evolution in the light of experience. Much will depend on the willingness and capacity of partners to contribute. This is a question of active, positive engagement in a spirit of mutual cooperation, not simply a matter of resources, though those, too, will be needed.

PFP offers a partnership of opportunity. We, in the Alliance, will do our share to ensure that the Partnership reaches the potential it promises for enchanting the security and stability in Europe that all of us so ardently seek.

DOCUMENT 42

THE DAYTON PEACE AGREEMENT, 1995*

Yugoslavia, a nation of diverse ethnic and religious regions, came under the rule of Josef Broz Tito and a communist regime following the Second World War. After his death in 1985, the country faced increasing tensions between competing regions and in 1991 the first area declared its independence. Other sections soon followed. This led to a civil war in the central and southern regions that ravaged the population and was characterized by the use of "ethnic cleansing" involving atrocities against civilians for their ethnic identity and religion. International efforts to bring these conditions to an end finally resulted in an agreement signed in Dayton, Ohio, in November 1995, by the leaders of the central and southern regions. International peace-keepers attempted to keep the warring parties from further hostilities, but it was an uneasy peace that only barely maintained a degree of stability. By the later 1990s, further violence erupted which led to the use of NATO force in

* http://www.state.gov/www/regions/eur/bosnia/bossumm.html.

1999 against the repressive "ethnic cleansing" policies of the government of President Slobodan Milosevic. The following excerpts come from an official summary of the 1995 agreement, initialled in Dayton on November 21, 1995 and formally adopted by the several governments in Paris on December 14, 1995.

γ   γ   γ

The Dayton Proximity Talks culminated in the initialing of a General Framework Agreement for Peace in Bosnia and Herzegovina. It was initiated by the Republic of Bosnia and Herzegovina, the Republic of Croatia and the Federal Republic of Yugoslavia (FRY). The Agreement was witnessed by representatives of the Contact Group nations—the United States, Britain, France, Germany, and Russia—and the European Union Special Negotiator. . . .

General Framework Agreement

[a] Bosnia and Herzegovina, Croatia and the Federal Republic of Yugoslavia agree to fully respect the sovereign equality of one another and to settle disputes by peaceful means.

[b] The FRY and Bosnia and Herzegovina recognize each other, and agree to discuss further aspects of their mutual recognition.

[c] The parties agree to fully respect and promote fulfillment of the commitments made in the various Annexes, and they obligate themselves to respect human rights and the rights of refugees and displaced persons.

[d] The parties agree to cooperate fully with all entities, including those authorized by the United Nations [UN] Security Council, in implementing the peace settlement and investigating and prosecuting war crimes and other violations of international humanitarian law.

Annex 1-A: Military Aspects

[a] The cease-fire that began with the agreement of October 5, 1995 will continue.

[b] Foreign combatant forces currently in Bosnia are to be withdrawn within 30 days.

[c] The parties must complete withdrawal of forces behind a zone of separation of approximately 4 km within an agreed period. Special provisions relate to Sarajevo and Gorazde.

[d] As a confidence-building measure, the parties agree to withdraw

heavy weapons and forces to cantonment/barracks areas within an agreed period and to demobilize forces which cannot be accommodated in those areas.

[e] The agreement invites into Bosnia and Herzegovina a multinational military Implementation Force, the IFOR, under the command of NATO, with a grant of authority from the UN.

[f] The IFOR will have the right to monitor and help ensure compliance with the agreement on military aspects and fulfill certain supporting tasks. The IFOR will have the right to carry out its mission vigorously, including with the use of force as necessary. It will have unimpeded freedom of movement, control over airspace, and status of forces protection.

[g] A Joint Military Commission is established to be chaired by the IFOR Commander. Persons under indictment by the International War Crimes Tribunal cannot participate.

[h] Information on mines, military personnel, weaponry and other items must be provided to the Joint Military Commission within agreed periods.

[i] All combatants and civilians must be released and transferred without delay in accordance with a plan to be developed by the International Committee of the Red Cross [ICRC].

Annex 1-B: Regional Stabilization

[a] The Republic of Bosnia and Herzegovina, the Federation and the Bosnian Serb Republic must begin negotiations within 7 days, under Organization for Security and Cooperation in Europe (OSCE) auspices, with the objective of agreeing on confidence-building measures within 45 days. These could include, for example, restrictions on military deployments and exercises, notification of military activities and exchange of data.

[b] The three parties, as well as Croatia and the Federal Republic of Yugoslavia, agree not to import arms for 90 days and not to import any heavy weapons, heavy weapons ammunition, mines, military aircraft, and helicopters for 180 days or until an arms control agreement takes effect.

[c] All five parties must begin negotiations within 30 days, under OSCE auspices, to agree on numerical limits on holding of tanks, artillery, armored combat vehicles, combat aircraft and attack helicopters.

[d] If the parties fail to establish limits on these categories within 180

days, the agreement provides for specified limits to come into force for the parties.

[e] The OSCE will organize and conduct negotiations to establish a regional balance in and around the former Yugoslavia. . . .

Annex 3: Elections

[a] Free and fair, internationally supervised elections will be conducted within six to nine months for the Presidency and House of Representatives of Bosnia and Herzegovina, for the House of Representatives of the Federation and the National Assembly and presidency of the Bosnian Serb Republic, and, if feasible, for local offices.

[b] Refugees and persons displaced by the conflict will have the right to vote (including by absentee ballot) in their original place of residence if they choose to do so.

[c] The parties must create conditions in which free and fair elections can be held by protecting the right to vote in secret and ensuring freedom of expression and the press.

[d] The OSCE is requested to supervise the preparation and conduct of these elections.

[e] All citizens of Bosnia and Herzegovina aged 18 or older listed on the 1991 Bosnian census are eligible to vote. . . .

Annex 5: Arbitration

[a] The Federation and the Bosnian Serb Republic agree to enter into reciprocal commitments to engage in binding arbitration to resolve disputes between them, and they agree to design and implement a system of arbitration.

Annex 6: Human Rights

[a] The agreement guarantees internationally recognized human rights and fundamental freedoms for all persons within Bosnia and Herzegovina.

[b] A Commission on Human Rights, composed of a Human Rights Ombudsman and a Human Rights Chamber (court), is established.

[c] The Ombudsman is authorized to investigate human rights violations, issue findings, and bring and participate in proceedings before the Human Rights Chamber.

[d] The Human Rights Chamber is authorized to hear and decide human rights claims and to issue binding decisions.

[e] The parties agree to grant UN human rights agencies, the OSCE, the International Tribunal and other organizations full access to monitor the human rights situation.

Annex 7: Refugees and Displaced Persons

[a] The agreement grants refugees and displaced persons the right to safely return home and regain lost property, or to obtain just compensation.

[b] A Commission for Displaced Persons and Refugees will decide on return of real property or compensation, with the authority to issue final decisions.

[c] All persons are granted the right to move freely throughout the country, without harassment or discrimination.

[d] The parties commit to cooperate with the ICRC in finding all missing persons. . . .

Annex 11: International Police Task Force

[a] The UN is requested to establish a UN International Police Task Force (IPTF) to carry out various tasks, including training and advising local law enforcement personnel, as well as monitoring and inspecting law enforcement activities and facilities.

[b] The IPTF will by headed by a Commissioner appointed by the UN Secretary General.

[c] IPTF personnel must report any credible information on human rights violations to the Human Rights Commission, the International Tribunal or other appropriate organizations.

Agreement on Initialing the General Framework Agreement

[a] In this agreement, which was signed at Dayton, Bosnia and Herzegovina, Croatia and the Federal Republic of Yugoslavia agree that the negotiations have been completed. They, and the Entities they represent, commit themselves to signature of the General Framework Agreement and its Annexes in Paris.

[b] They also agreed that the initialing of the General Framework Agreement and its Annexes in Dayton expresses their consent to be bound by these agreements.

DOCUMENT 43

THE NATO-RUSSIA FOUNDING ACT, 1997*

In the aftermath of the breakup of the Soviet Union in 1991, the end of the communist regime in that country, the abolition of the Warsaw Pact, and improved world conditions in the 1990s, the North Atlantic Treaty Organization (NATO) and Russia undertook a series of negotiated steps to work more cooperatively in their relationship as compared to the confrontational environment of the Cold War years. Russia joined the NATO-sponsored "Partnership for Peace" in 1994, and this was expanded in May 1997 with a more extensive and significant agreement, "The Founding Act on Mutual Relations, Cooperation and Security between NATO and the Russian Federation." The following are excerpts of the official text, signed in Paris on May 27, 1997.

γ   γ   γ

The North Atlantic Treaty Organization and its member States, on the one hand, and the Russian Federation, on the other hand, hereinafter referred to as NATO and Russia, based on an enduring political commitment undertaken at the highest political level, will build together a lasting and inclusive peace in the Euro-Atlantic area on the principles of democracy and cooperative security.

NATO and Russia do not consider each other as adversaries. They share the goal of overcoming the vestiges of earlier confrontation and competition and of strengthening mutual trust and cooperation. The present Act reaffirms the determination of NATO and Russia to give concrete substance to their shared commitment to build a stable, peaceful and undivided Europe, whole and free, to the benefit of all its peoples. Making this commitment at the highest political level marks the beginning of a fundamentally new relationship between NATO and Russia. They intend to develop, on the basis of common interest, reciprocity and transparency a strong, stable and enduring partnership. This Act defines the goals and mechanism of consultation, cooperation, joint decision-making and joint action that will constitute the core of the mutual relations between NATO and Russia.

* http://www.nato.int/docu/basictxt/fndact-a.htm.

NATO has undertaken a historic transformation—a process that will continue. In 1991 the Alliance revised its strategic doctrine to take account of the new security environment in Europe. Accordingly, NATO has radically reduced and continues the adaptation of its conventional and nuclear forces. While preserving the capability to meet the commitments undertaken in the Washington Treaty, NATO has expanded and will continue to expand its political functions, and take on new missions of peacekeeping and crisis management in support of the United Nations (UN) and the Organisation for Security and Cooperation in Europe (OSCE), such as in Bosnia and Herzegovina, to address new security challenges in close association with other countries and international organisations. NATO is in the process of developing the European Security and Defence Identity (ESDI) within the Alliance. It will continue to develop a broad and dynamic pattern of cooperation with OSCE participating States in particular through the Partnership for Peace and is working with Partner countries on the initiative to establish a Euro-Atlantic Partnership Council. NATO member States have decided to examine NATO's Strategic Concept to ensure that it is fully consistent with Europe's new security situation and challenges.

Russia is continuing the building of a democratic society and the realisation of its political and economic transformation. It is developing the concept of its national security and revising its military doctrine to ensure that they are fully consistent with new security realities. Russia has carried out deep reductions in its armed forces, has withdrawn its forces on an unprecedented scale from the countries of Central and Eastern Europe and the Baltic countries and withdrawn all its nuclear weapons back to its own national territory. Russia is committed to further reducing its conventional and nuclear forces. It is actively participating in peacekeeping operations in support of the UN and the OSCE, as well as in crisis management in different areas of the world. Russia is contributing to the multinational forces in Bosnia and Herzegovina.

1. Principles.
Proceeding from the principles that the security of all states in the Euro-Atlantic community is indivisible, NATO and Russia will work together to contribute to the establishment in Europe of common and comprehensive security based on the allegiance to shared values, commitments and norms of behaviour in the interests of all states. NATO

and Russia will help to strengthen the Organisation for Security and Cooperation in Europe, including developing further its role as a primary instrument in preventive diplomacy, conflict prevention, crisis management, post-conflict rehabilitation and regional security cooperation, as well as in enhancing its operational capabilities to carry out these tasks. The OSCE, as the only pan-European security organisation, has a key role in European peace and stability. In strengthening the OSCE, NATO and Russia will cooperate to prevent any possibility of returning to a Europe of division and confrontation, or the isolation of any state. . . .

NATO and Russia start from the premise that the shared objective of strengthening security and stability in the Euro-Atlantic area for the benefit of all countries requires a response to new risks and challenges, such as aggressive nationalism, proliferation of nuclear, biological and chemical weapons, terrorism, persistent abuse of human rights and of the rights of persons belonging to national minorities and unresolved territorial disputes, which pose a threat to common peace, prosperity and stability. . . .

In implementing the provisions in this Act, NATO and Russia will observe in good faith their obligations under international law and international instruments, including the obligations of the United Nations Charter and the provisions of the Universal Declaration on Human Rights as well as their commitments under the Helsinki Final Act and subsequent OSCE documents, including the Charter of Paris and the documents adopted at the Lisbon OSCE Summit.

To achieve the aims of this Act, NATO and Russia will base their relations on a shared commitment to the following principles:
—development, on the basis of transparency, of a strong, stable, enduring and equal partnership and of cooperation to strengthen security and stability in the Euro-Atlantic area;
—acknowledgement of the vital role that democracy, political pluralism, the rule of law, and respect for human rights and civil liberties and the development of free market economies play in the development of common prosperity and comprehensive security;
—refraining from the threat or use of force against each other as well as against any other state, its sovereignty, territorial integrity or political independence in any manner inconsistent with the United Nations

Charter and with the Declaration of Principles Guiding Relations Between Participating States contained in the Helsinki Final Act [1975];
—respect for sovereignty, independence and territorial integrity of all
states and their inherent right to choose the means to ensure their own
security, the inviolability of borders and peoples' right of self-determination as enshrined in the Helsinki Final Act and other OSCE documents;
—mutual transparency in creating and implementing defence policy
and military doctrines;
—prevention of conflicts and settlement of disputes by peaceful means
in accordance with UN and OSCE principles;
—support, on a case-by-case basis, of peacekeeping operations carried
out under the authority of the UN Security Council or the responsibility
of the OSCE.

II. Mechanism for Consultation and Cooperation, the NATO-Russian
Permanent Joint Council.
To carry out the activities and aims provided for by this Act and to develop common approaches to European security and to political problems, NATO and Russia will create the NATO-Russia Permanent Joint
Council. The central objectives of this Permanent Joint Council will be
to build increasing levels of trust, unity of purpose and habits of consultation and cooperation between NATO and Russia, in order to enhance each other's security and that of all nations in the Euro-Atlantic
area and diminish the security of none. If disagreements arise, NATO
and Russia will endeavour to settle them on the basis of goodwill and
mutual respect within the framework of political consultations.

The Permanent Joint Council will provide a mechanism for consultations, coordination and, to the maximum extent possible, where appropriate, for joint decisions and joint action with respect to security issues
of common concern. The consultations will not extend to internal matters of either NATO, NATO member States or Russia. The shared objective of NATO and Russia is to identify and pursue as many opportunities for joint action as possible. As the relationship develops, they
expect that additional opportunities for joint action will emerge. . . .

The activities of the Permanent Joint Council will be built upon the
principles of reciprocity and transparency. In the course of their consultations and cooperation, NATO and Russia will inform each other

regarding the respective security-related challenges they face and the measures that each intends to take to address them. Provisions of this Act do not provide NATO or Russia, in any way, with a right of veto over the actions of the other nor do they infringe upon or restrict the rights of NATO or Russia to independent decision-making and action. They cannot be used as a means to disadvantage the interests of other states.

The Permanent Joint Council will meet at various levels and in different forms, according to the subject matter and the wishes of NATO and Russia The Permanent Joint Council will meet at the level of Foreign Ministers and at the level of Defence Ministers twice annually, and also monthly at the level of ambassadors/permanent representatives to the North Atlantic Council. The Permanent Joint Council may also meet, as appropriate, at the level of the Heads of State and Government.

The Permanent Joint Council may establish committees or working groups for individual subjects or areas of cooperation on an ad hoc or permanent basis, as appropriate.

Under the auspices of the Permanent Joint Council, military representatives and Chiefs of Staff will also meet, meetings of Chiefs of Staff will take place no less than twice a year, and also monthly at military representatives level. Meetings of military experts may be convened, as appropriate.

The Permanent Joint Council will be chaired jointly by the Secretary General of NATO, a representative of one of the NATO member States on a rotation basis, and a representative of Russia. To support the work of the Permanent Joint Council, NATO and Russia will establish the necessary administrative structures. Russia will establish a Mission to NATO headed by a representative at the rank of Ambassador. A senior military representative and his staff will be part of this Mission for the purposes of the military cooperation. NATO retains the possibility of establishing an appropriate presence in Moscow, the modalities of which remain to be determined.

The agenda for regular sessions will be established jointly. Organisational arrangements and rules of procedure for the Permanent Joint

Council will be worked out. These arrangements will be in place for the inaugural meeting of the Permanent Joint Council which will be held no later than four months after the signature of this act. . . .

DOCUMENT 44

HAVEL ON THE POST-COMMUNIST ERA, 1997*

Vaclav Havel (born 1936) was a Czech intellectual and playwright who spoke out against the stultifying atmosphere of the communist regime in Czechoslovakia. Like other reform supporters, he was persecuted by the authorities and imprisoned. With the overthrow of the communist government in November 1989, he was elected the country's president. In the following years, however, the nation faced an uneven transition to a democratic system. Czechoslovakia in 1993 divided into two separate states: the Czech Republic and Slovakia. Social problems and economic challenges also showed the fragile nature of the new era. President Havel spoke of the issues that had to be faced in order to bring the country into the post-communist era based on justice, protection of individual rights, and responsibile citizenship. The following, excerpts from a lengthy speech made to the parliament in 1997, broadly reveal what he believed the Czech people had to do to face the future.

γ   γ   γ

With a certain amount of simplification, we can say that the life of our society—just as the life of any society, in any situation,—has two sides, even though one can always be seen through the other somehow.

One of the sides of our society's life is made up of prevailing human occupations: people go to work, and do well, or less well in their jobs; engage in private business; get married or divorced; beget children or remain childless; form a variety of associations; make holiday trips to foreign countries; read books or watch television; and those who are younger than most of us go to discotheques. I think that the everyday life—for all you may say—is now far better and more colourful than it

* http://pes.eunet.cz/97/50/0050ar15.htm.

was in those times when almost everything was forbidden, and almost everyone was afraid to say aloud what they thought.

There is, however, also a second side of our life, one that we may perhaps describe as peoples' attitude toward their state, toward their social system, toward the climate of public life, toward politics. It seems to me that this is what we should concern ourselves with before everything else. We should inquire into the reasons why this side of life looks so gloomy now, and think about ways in which we could brighten it up a little before long.

This side of life indeed shows a rather gloomy face at the moment. Many people—the opinion polls corroborate this—are disturbed, disappointed or even disgusted by the general condition of society in our country. Many believe that—democracy or no democracy—power is again in the hands of untrustworthy figures whose primary concern is their personal advancement instead of the interests of the people. Many are convinced that honest business people fare badly while fraudulent nouveaux riches get the green light. The prevalent opinion is that it pays off in this country to lie and to steal; that many politicians and civil servants are corruptible; that political parties—though they all declare honest intentions in lofty words—are covertly manipulated by suspicious financial groupings. Many wonder why—after eight years of building a market economy—our economic performance leaves much to be desired, and even compels the government to patch together packages of austerity measures; why we choke in smog, when so much money is said to be spent on environment protection; why all prices, including rents and electricity tariffs, have to go up without a corresponding increase in pensions or other social welfare benefits; why they must fear for their safety when walking in the centers of our cities at night; why almost nothing is being built except banks, hotels and homes for the rich; etc. etc. An increasing number of people are disgusted by politics which they hold responsible—and rightly so—for all these adverse developments. As as consequence, they have begun to feel suspicious of us all, or even take an aversion to us—notwithstanding the fact that they freely elected us for our offices.

You need not be afraid that I will undertake a comprehensive sociological analysis of these warning occurrences. I will simply mention two causes, or rather sets of causes, of this situation.

The first of them is what I would call the "historical" cause. It is, in fact, the Czech version of a phenomenon that has made itself felt, in different forms and with differing intensity, in all the countries that rid themselves of communism. We may perhaps call it post-communist morass. Something like that was bound to come—every person of sound judgement must have known that. Hardly anybody, however, foresaw how deep, serious and protracted it would be. The collapse of communism brought down, virtually overnight, also a whole structure of values that had been kept in existence for several decades, and with it the way of life based on that construction. The "time of certainties"—that were limited and dull, even suicidal to society, but still represented a certainty of a kind—was suddenly replaced by a time of freedom. Given the previous experience, it was inevitable that many took this new freedom to be boundless. The new life, which held dozens of temptations, also made entirely new demands on individual responsibility—in a measure that many find hard to bear. I have compared this strange state of mind to a post-prison psychosis experienced by those who—after having been constrained for years to a narrow corridor of strict and detailed rules—suddenly find themselves in an expanse of freedom that is strange to them. The new condition made them believe that everything is permitted; at the same time, however, it thrusts upon them the tremendous burden of having to make their own decisions, and accept responsibility for those decisions. It is my firm belief and hope that the young generation—those who grew up after the fall of communism—will not be affected by this terrible post-communist syndrome, and I am looking forward to the time when these people take over the administration of public affairs. That time has not yet come; we are still living in a situation which makes us wonder how long it will take society to adapt to the new, more natural conditions of life, and how deeply the totalitarian era affected our souls.

However, it would not be honest to ascribe all blame—in a way that was so well known to the Marxists—to some blind laws of history. A no less important, or maybe an even more important, role is played here by the second set of causes—by what we have caused ourselves. Saying we, I refer to the whole body of post-November [1989] politicians, and particularly to political representatives of the independent Czech Republic, that is, all of us who have had an influence on the fate of this country in the past five years. I intentionally refrain from making distinctions according to the measure of responsibility or guilt, although it is clear that some deserve more blame than others. But that is not the point now. First of all, it is necessary to identify our faults.

It appears to me that our main fault was pride. Because of the fact that the transformation process progressed in our country practically continuously since November 1989, without being impeded by any major political changes, we really got, in some respects, farther than others— or at least it seemed so. Apparently, this went to our heads. We behaved like a spoiled child in a family, or like the top of the class who believe they can give themselves an air of superiority and be everyone else's teacher. Oddly enough, this pride was combined with a kind of provincialism or parochialism. We disrupted, for example, our close political cooperation with our nearest neighbours—that which used to be called Visegrad—because we thought we were superior to the rest of the group. Now that we have been invited, together with these nations, to join the European integration grouping, and that we see they have gotten farther than we have in a number of respects, we must exert a great deal of effort to restore that cooperation. Many of us ridiculed all those who spoke about global responsibility in the interconnected civilization of today's world, and maintained that a tiny country like our own should deal only with our tiny Czech problems. Now, we must go to great lengths to make it clear to our own citizens that we can be granted security guarantees only when we are prepared to take our share of responsibility for Europe and the world, and to convince the North Atlantic Alliance [NATO] that we are aware of that. . . .

DOCUMENT 45

NATO ADDS NEW MEMBERS, 1997–1999*

The North Atlantic Treaty Organization (NATO) was established in 1949, composed of twelve original members. Its primary objective was to be a defensive Western alliance of European and North American states to resist possible Soviet aggression. In later years, new members increased the size of the alliance: Greece and Turkey (1951), West Germany (1955), and Spain

* http://www.usinfo.state.gov/usa.infousa/laws/treaties/nato.htm.

(1981). A major step in the continued growth of the organization came in 1999 with the addition of three central European states that formerly had been members of the Warsaw Pact, the communist counterpart to NATO: the Czech Republic, Hungary, and Poland. Those nations, adopting democratic regimes in the aftermath of their years under communist rule, applied for NATO membership in the 1990s and their applications were accepted in 1997. Approval by all existing NATO member governments was required, along with fulfilling other criteria for admission. Formal entry of the three states into the alliance occurred in March 1999 at the time of the 50th anniversary of NATO's creation. The document below illustrates a portion of the approval process as President Bill Clinton asked the U.S. Senate to approve the procedural agreements that had been completed to that time. He provided the broad rationale for the entry of three new members. The references to Bosnia relate to NATO's efforts to bring the 1992–1995 civil war in the region to an end through the presence of the alliance's military forces and diplomatic efforts that led to a peace agreement in November 1995. Also note his comments to reassure Russia that this enlargement did not signify NATO's opposition to Russian interests.

γ   γ   γ

Letter of Transmittal
The White House
February 11, 1998

To the Senate of the United States:

I transmit herewith Protocols to the North Atlantic Treaty of 1949 on the accession of Poland, Hungary, and the Czech Republic. These Protocols were opened for signature at Brussels on December 16, 1997, and signed on behalf of the United States of America and the other parties to the North Atlantic Treaty. I request the advice and consent of the Senate to the ratification of these documents, and transmit for the Senate's information the report made to me by the Secretary of State regarding this matter.

The accession of Poland, Hungary, and the Czech Republic to the North Atlantic Treaty Organization (NATO) will improve the ability of the United States to protect and advance our interests in the transatlantic area. The end of the Cold War changed the nature of the threats to this region, but not the fact that Europe's peace, stability, and well-being are vital to our own national security. The addition of these well-qualified democracies, which have demonstrated their commitment to the values of freedom and the security of the broader region, will help deter potential threats to Europe, deepen the continent's stability, bolster its democratic advances, erase its artificial division, and strengthen an Alliance that has proved it effectiveness during and since the Cold War.

NATO is not the only instrument in our efforts to help build a new and undivided Europe, but it is our most important contributor to peace and security for the region. NATO's steadfastness during the long years of the Cold War, its performance in the mission it has led in Bosnia, the strong interest of a dozen new European democracies in becoming members, and the success of the Alliance's Partnership for Peace program all underscore the continuing vitality of the Alliance and the Treaty that brought it into existence.

NATO's mission in Bosnia is of particular importance. No other multinational institution possessed the military capabilities and political cohesiveness necessary to bring an end to the fighting in the former Yugoslavia—Europe's worst conflict since World War II—and to give the people of that region a chance to build a lasting peace. Our work in Bosnia is not yet complete, but we should be thankful that NATO existed to unite Allies and partners in this determined common effort. Similarly, we should welcome steps such as the Alliance's enlargement that can strengthen its ability to meet future challenges, beginning with NATO's core mission of collective defense and other missions that we and our Allies may choose to pursue.

The three states that NATO now proposes to add as full members will make the Alliance stronger while helping to enlarge Europe's zone of democratic stability. Poland, Hungary, and the Czech Republic have been leaders in Central Europe's dramatic transformation over the past decade and already are a part of NATO's community of values. They each played pivotal roles in the overthrow of communist rule and repression, and they each proved equal to the challenge of comprehensive democratic and market reform. Together, they have helped to make Central Europe the continent's most robust zone of economic growth.

All three of these states will be security producers for the Alliance and not merely security consumers. They have demonstrated this through the accords they have reached with neighboring states, the contributions they have made to the mission of Bosnia, the forces they plan to commit to the Alliance, and the military modernization programs they have already begun and pledge to continue in the years to come at their own expense. These three states will strengthen NATO through the addition of military resources, strategic depth, and the prospect of greater stability in Europe's central region. American troops have worked alongside soldiers from each of these nations in earlier times, in the case of the Poles, dating back to our own Revolutionary War. Our cooperation with the Poles, Hungarians, and Czechs has contributed to our security in the past, and our Alliance with them will contribute to our security in the years to come.

The purpose of NATO's enlargement extends beyond the security of these three states, however, and entails a process encompassing more than their admission to the Alliance. Accordingly, these first new members should not and will not be the last. No qualified European democracy is ruled out as a future member. The Alliance has agreed to review the process of enlargement at its 1999 summit in Washington. As we prepare for that summit, I look forward to discussing this matter with my fellow NATO leaders. The process of enlargement, combined with the Partnership for Peace program, the Euro-Atlantic Partnership Council, the NATO-Russia Founding Act, and NATO's new charter with Ukraine, signify NATO's commitment to avoid any new division of Europe, and to contribute to its progressive integration.

A democratic Russia is and should be a part of that new Europe. With bipartisan congressional support, my Administration and my predecessor's have worked with our Allies to support political and economic reform in Russia and the other newly independent states and to increase the bonds between them and the rest of Europe. NATO's enlargement and other adaptions are consistent, not at odds, with that policy. NATO has repeatedly demonstrated that it does not threaten Russia and that it seeks closer and more cooperative relations. We and our Allies welcomed the participation of Russian forces in the mission in Bosnia.

NATO most clearly signaled its interest in a constructive relationship through the signing in May 1997 of the NATO-Russia Founding Act. That Act, and the Permanent Joint Council it created, help to ensure that if Russia seeks to build a positive and peaceful future within Europe, NATO will be a full partner in that enterprise. I understand it will require time for the Russian people to gain a new understanding of NATO. The Russian people, in turn, must understand that an open door policy with regard to the addition of new members is an element of a new NATO. In this way, we will build a new and more stable Europe of which Russia is an integral part.

I therefore propose the ratification of these Protocols with every expectation that we can continue to pursue productive cooperation with the Russian Federation. I am encouraged that President Yeltsin has pledged his government's commitment to additional progress on nuclear and conventional arms control measures. At our summit in Helsinki, for example, we agreed that once START II has entered into force we will begin negotiations on a START III accord that can achieve even deeper cuts in our strategic arsenals. Similarly, Russia's ratification of the Chemical Weapons Convention last year demonstrated that cooperation on a range of security issues will continue.

The Protocols of accession that I transmit to you constitute a decision of great consequence, and they involve solemn security commitments. The addition of new states also will entail financial costs. While those costs will be manageable and broadly shared with our current and new Allies, they nonetheless represent a sacrifice by the American people.

Successful ratification of these Protocols demands not only the Senate's advice and consent required by our Constitution, but also the broader, bipartisan support of the American people and their representatives. For that reason, it is encouraging that congressional leaders in both parties and both chambers have long advocated NATO's enlargement. I have endeavored to make the Congress an active partner in this process. I was pleased that a bipartisan group of Senators and Representatives accompanied the U.S. delegation at the NATO summit in Madrid last July. Officials at all levels of my Administration have consulted closely with the relevant committees and with the bipartisan Senate NATO Observer Group. It is my hope that this pattern of consultation and cooperation will ensure that NATO and our broader European policies continue to have the sustained bipartisan support that was so instrumental to their success throughout the decades of the Cold War.

The American people today are the direct beneficiaries of the extraordinary sacrifices made by our fellow citizens in the many theaters of that "long twilight struggle," and in the two world wars that preceded it. Those efforts aimed in large part to create across the breadth of Europe a lasting, democratic peace. The enlargement of NATO represents an indispensable part of today's program to finish building such a peace, and therefore to repay a portion of the debt we owe to those who went before us in the quest for freedom and security.

The rise of new challenges in other regions does not in any way diminish the necessity of consolidating the increased level of security that Europe has attained at such high cost. To the contrary, our policy in Europe, including the Protocols I transmit herewith, can help preserve today's more favorable security environment in the transatlantic area, thus making it possible to focus attention and resources elsewhere while providing us with additional Allies and partners to help share our security burdens.

The century we are now completing has been the bloodiest in all of human history. Its lessons should be clear to us: the wisdom of deterrence, the value of strong Alliances, the potential for overcoming past divisions, and the imperative of American engagement in Europe. The NATO Alliance is one of the most important embodiments of these truths, and it is in the interest of the United States to strengthen this proven institution and adapt it to a new era. The addition to this Alliance of Poland, Hungary, and the Czech Republic is an essential part of that program. It will help build a Europe that can be integrated, democratic, free, and at peace for the first time in its history. It can help ensure that we and our allies and our partners will enjoy greater security and freedom in the century that is about to begin.

I therefore recommend that the Senate give prompt advice and consent to ratification of these historic Protocols.

William J. Clinton

DOCUMENT 46

NATO ACTS AGAINST YUGOSLAVIA, 1999*

The nation of Yugoslavia fragmented into its constituent parts (Slovenia, Croatia, Bosnia, Serbia and Macedonia) in the 1991–1995 period, unleashing conflict and devastation in a vicious civil war in many areas. The Dayton Peace Accord of 1995 attempted to end the fighting, but this region in southeastern Europe continued to be very unstable. Toward the end of the decade Serbia, asserting that it represented the Federal Republic of Yugoslavia (FRY), began a deliberate and hostile policy against the population of Kosovo, a province in southwestern Serbia. Belgrade's repressive actions against the Kosovar population were motivated by ethnic, religious, and historical factors. Centuries-old hostility between Orthodox Christians in Serbia and the Muslim population in Kosovo intensified the crisis. Albania, a predominantly Muslim state located adjacent to Kosovo, also became involved in this deteriorating situation. International bodies as the United Nations, the Organization for Security and Cooperation in Europe (OSCE), the European Union (EU), and the North Atlantic Treaty Organization (NATO), along with efforts of individual governments as the United States, unsuccessfully sought to persuade the Yugoslav government in Belgrade under President Slobodan Milosevic to end its destructive actions that an international court later classified as genocide. Those diplomatic failures in 1998 and early 1999, after months of fruitless negotiations, convinced NATO that direct action had to be taken to protect the Kosovar population. It issued the following statement on April 24, 1999 to justify NATO military forces that began combat operations against Serbia. These military operations lasted from April to June 1999, until the Belgrade authorities agreed to end its ruthless and repressive policies.

γ　　　　　　　γ　　　　　　　γ

* By permission of *NATO Review*, 47 (Summer 1999), pp. D1–D2.

Statement on Kosovo issued by the Heads of State and Government participating in the meeting of the North Atlantic Council in Washington DC on 23 and 24 April 1999.

1. The crisis in Kosovo represents a fundamental challenge to the values for which NATO has stood since its foundation: democracy, human rights and the rule of law. It is the culmination of a deliberate policy of oppression, ethnic cleansing and violence pursued by the Belgrade regime under the direction of President Milosevic. We will not allow this campaign of terror to succeed. NATO is determined to prevail.

2. NATO's military action against the Federal Republic of Yugoslavia (FRY) supports the political aims of the international community, which were reaffirmed in recent statements by the UN Secretary-General and the European Union: a peaceful, multi-ethnic and democratic Kosovo where all its people can live in security and enjoy universal human rights and freedoms on an equal basis.

3. Our military actions are directed not at the Serb people but at the policies of the regime in Belgrade, which has repeatedly rejected all efforts to solve the crisis peacefully. President Milosevic must:

[a] Ensure a verifiable stop to all military action and the immediate ending of violence and repression in Kosovo;

[b] Withdraw from Kosovo his military, police and paramilitary forces;

[c] Agree to the stationing in Kosovo of an international military presence;

[d] Agree to the unconditional and safe return of all refugees and displaced persons, and unhindered access to them by humanitarian aid organisations; and

[e] Provide credible assurance of his willingness to work for the establishment of a political framework agreement based on the Rambouillet accords.

4. There can be no compromise on these conditions. As long as Belgrade fails to meet the legitimate demands of the international community and continues to inflict immense human suffering, Alliance air operations against the Yugoslav war machine will continue. We hold President Milosevic and the Belgrade leadership responsible for the safety of all Kosovar citizens. We will fulfill our promise to the Kosovar people that they can return to their homes and live in peace and security.

5. We are intensifying NATO's military actions to increase the pressure on Belgrade. Allied governments are putting in place additional re-

sources to tighten the constraints on the Belgrade regime. These include intensified implementation of economic sanctions, and an embargo on petroleum products on which we welcome the EU lead. We have directed our Defence Ministers to determine ways that NATO can contribute to halting the delivery of war material including by launching maritime operations, taking into account the possible consequences on Montenegro.

6. NATO is prepared to suspend its air strikes once Belgrade has unequivocally accepted the above mentioned conditions and demonstrably begun to withdraw its forces from Kosovo according to a precise and rapid timetable. This could follow the passage of a United Nations Security Council resolution, which we will seek, requiring the withdrawal of Serb forces and the demilitarisation of Kosovo and encompassing the deployment of an international military force to safeguard the swift return of all refugees and displaced persons as well as the establishment of an international provisional administration of Kosovo under which its people can enjoy substantial autonomy within the FRY. NATO remains ready to form the core of such an international military force. It would be multinational in character with contributions from non-NATO countries.

7. Russia has a particular responsibility in the United Nations and an important role to play in the search for a solution to the conflict in Kosovo. Such a solution must be based on the conditions of the international community as laid out above. President Milosevic's offers to date do not meet this test. We want to work constructively with Russia, in the spirit of the Founding Act.

8. The long–planned, unrestrained and continuing assault by Yugoslav military, police and paramilitary forces on Kosovars and the repression directed against other minorities of the FRY are aggravating the already massive humanitarian catastrophe. This threatens to destabilise the surrounding region.

9. NATO, its members and its Partners have responded to the humanitarian emergency and are intensifying their refugee and humanitarian relief operations in close cooperation with the UNHCR [United Nations High Commission for Refugees], the lead agency in this field, and with other relevant organisations. We will continue our assistance as long as necessary. NATO forces are making a major contribution to this task.

10. We pay tribute to the servicemen and women of NATO whose

courage and dedication are ensuring the success of our military and humanitarian operations.

11. Atrocities against the people of Kosovo by FRY military, police and paramilitary forces represent a flagrant violation of international law. Our governments will cooperate with the International Criminal Tribunal for the former Yugoslavia (ICTY) to support investigation of all those, including at the highest levels, responsible for war crimes and crimes against humanity.

12. We acknowledge and welcome the courageous support that states in the region are providing to our effort in Kosovo. The former Yugoslav Republic of Macedonia and Albania have played a particularly important role, not least in accepting hundreds of thousands of refugees from Kosovo. The states in the region are bearing substantial economic and social burdens stemming from the current conflict.

13. We will not tolerate threats by the Belgrade regime to the security of its neighbours. We will respond to such challenges by Belgrade to its neighbours resulting from the presence of NATO forces or their activities on their territory during this crisis.

14. We reaffirm our support for the territorial integrity and sovereignty of all countries in the region.

15. We reaffirm our strong support for the democratically elected government of Montenegro. Any move by Belgrade to undermine the government of President Djukanovic will have grave consequences. FRY forces should leave the demilitarised zone of Prevlaka immediately.

16. The objective of a free, prosperous, open and economically integrated Southeast Europe cannot be fully assured until the FRY embarks upon the transition to democracy. Accordingly, we express our support for the objective of a democratic FRY which protects the rights of all minorities, including those in Vojvodina and Sanjak, and promise to work for such change through and beyond the current conflict.

17. It is our aim to make stability in Southeast Europe a priority of our transatlantic agenda. Our governments will cooperate urgently through NATO as well as through the OSCE, and for those of us which are members, the European Union, to support the nations of Southeast Europe in forging a better future for their region—one based on democracy, justice, economic integration, and security cooperation.

DOCUMENT 47

BORIS YELTSIN'S RESIGNATION, 1999*

Elected President of the Russian Federation in 1991, Boris Yeltsin led his country in the period following the breakup of the Soviet Union. During these years Russia faced numerous political and economic difficulties in developing democratic values and institutions within a free-enterprise market economy. The social and psychological adjustments in this transition disoriented the population, many of whom missed the order and authoritarianism of the former communist system. Yeltsin was reelected to the presidency in 1996 for a second term. On December 31, 1999 he made a surprise television announcement that he was resigning immediately and took that opportunity to reflect on his country and his leadership in the post-communist period.

γ   γ   γ

Dear Russians!

A very short time remains before a magical date in our history. The year 2000 is approaching. A new century, a new millennium. We have all tried on this date. We have pondered, beginning in childhood, then having grown up, how old we would be in 2000, and how old our mothers would be and how old our children would be. At some point, this unusual New Year seemed so far away. Now this day is upon us.

Dear Friends! My dear ones! Today I am turning to you for the last time with New Year's greetings. But that's not all. Today I am turning to you for the last time as president of Russia. I have made a decision. I thought long and hard over it. Today, on the last day of the departing century, I am resigning.

I have heard many times that "Yeltsin will hang onto power by any means, he won't give it to anyone." That's a lie. But that's not the point. I have always said that I would not depart one bit from the Constitution. That parliamentary elections should take place in the constitutionally established terms. That was done. And I also wanted presidential elections to take place on time—in June 2000. This was very important for Russia. We are creating a very important precedent of a civilized, vol-

* Reprinted with permission of The Associated Press.

untary transfer of power, power from one president of Russia to another, newly elected one.

And still, I made a different decision. I am leaving. I am leaving earlier than the set term. I have understood that it was necessary for me to do this. Russia must enter the new millennium with new politicians, with new faces, with new, smart, strong, energetic people. And we who have been in power for many years already, we must go.

Seeing with what hope and faith people voted in the [December 1999] parliamentary elections for a new generation of politicians, I understood that I have completed the main thing of my life. Already, Russia will never return to the past. Now, Russia will always move only forward. And I should not interfere with this natural march of history. To hold on to power for another half-year, when the country has a strong man [Prime Minister Vladimir Putin] who is worthy of being president and with whom practically every Russian today ties his hopes for the future? Why should I interfere with him? Why wait still another half-year? No, that's not for me. It's simply not in my character.

Today, on this day that is so extraordinarily important for me, I want to say just a few more personal words than usual. I want to ask for your forgiveness. For the fact that many of the dreams we shared did not come true. And for the fact that what seemed simple to us turned out to be tormentingly difficult. I ask forgiveness for not justifying some hopes of those people who believed that at one stroke, in one spurt, we could leap from the gray, stagnant, totalitarian past into the light, rich, civilized future. I myself believed in this, that we could overcome everything in one spurt.

I turned out to be too naive in something. In some places, problems seemed to be too complicated. We forced our way forward through mistakes, through failures. Many people in this hard time experienced shock. But I want you to know. I have never said this. Today it's important for me to tell you. The pain of each of you has called forth pain in me, in my heart. Sleepless nights, tormenting worries—about what needed to be done, so that people could live more easily and better. I did not have any more important task. I am leaving. I did all I could—not according to my health, but on the basis of all the problems. A new generation is relieving me, a generation of those who can do more and better.

In accordance with the Constitution, as I resign, I have signed a decree placing the duties of the president of Russia on the head of government, Vladimir Vladimirovich Putin. For three months, again in accordance with the Constitution, he will be the head of state. And in three months, presidential elections will take place. I have always been certain of the surprising wisdom of Russians. That's why I don't doubt what choice you will make at the end of March 2000.

Bidding farewell, I want to tell each of you: Be happy. You deserve happiness. Your deserve happiness and calm. Happy New Year! Happy new century, my dear ones!

DOCUMENT 48

GERMANY AND THE HOLOCAUST, 2000*

The impact of the Holocaust continued long after the end of hostilities and defeat of the Nazi regime in 1945, as post-war Germany and the German people had to cope with the heritage of the inhumane atrocities committed against millions of Europeans. Germany has used its legal system, education, media and other means to deal with issues of responsibility, morality and tolerance, as part of reckoning with this dark episode of its history. The German government has taken many steps, financial and otherwise, to demonstrate its commitment that such behavior will not reoccur. The following are excerpts of a speech given by Joschka Fischer, the Minister of Foreign Affairs and Vice-Chancellor of the Federal Republic of Germany, to the World Jewish Congress on September 11, 2000. His title was "Remembrance and Responsibility: There is No 'Moral Closure' for the Holocaust."

γ   γ   γ

I would like to thank you for inviting me as German Foreign Minister to be with you this evening and for asking me to address you. After all

* By permission of the Federal Republic of Germany.

the atrocities committed by Germany against European Jews during
Hitler's barbarous anti-Semitic dictatorship, this evening's motto "Partners in History" cannot apply to Germany. I therefore appreciate all the
more the awareness of our joint responsibility to keep alive the memories, which for democratic Germany are, at the same time, a continuing
obligation towards the future. Anti-Semitism, Neo-Nazism and racism
must never more be given a chance to thrive anywhere, least of all, however, in democratic Germany.

To this very day it is immensely difficult for us Germans, especially for
the younger generations who must take on this national legacy, to come
to terms with our country's moral and historical guilt for the Shoa. Of
course, it must not be forgotten that the memory of Hitler's terrible
genocide of European Jews is a much greater burden on the survivors
and their children and grandchildren.

Allow me to say a few personal words. My own political awareness began with the key German question which children of my generation
asked their parents. A question for which I have no answer to this day
and which to this day is a source of deep shame for democratic Germany: How could Hitler's criminal obsession, his genocidal anti-Semitism, his immeasurable hatred of all Jewish people, prevail in our, in my
country? Why did the majority of Germans at that time, our parents'
generation, allow this crime against humanity to happen, and why did
many of them participate in Hitler's extermination of the Jews? We, the
young and the not so young, have inherited this burden. We know that
we cannot cast it off. We cannot leave our history behind us. . . . For an
old Jewish saying teaches us that the desire to forget prolongs the exile
and the secret of redemption is to remember.

First of all, we remember the six million murdered sons and daughters
of the Jewish people. We remember the other victims of Hitler's racist
barbarity, war and Nazi violence. We remember the surviving victims.
But this also holds a lesson for us. When Germany sent its Jewish citizens from platform 17 at Berlin-Grunewald station and countless other
platforms to Auschwitz and other death camps and stole their property,
it deprived itself, its culture and society in a terrible manner which is
still painfully felt today. The murderous anti-Semitism of the Nazis not
only drove out and murdered a large portion of German and European

Jewry, but also destroyed a flourishing, centuries-old German and European culture. This gap has not been filled to this day and remains a painful loss.

However, keeping alive memories also means shouldering responsibility for our own, for our German history. The origins of today's German democracy and how it perceives itself can only be understood against the background of the Holocaust. . . . The lesson to be learned is clear and unambiguous: never again should this absolute minimum of civilized behavior, respect for human dignity, be violated. This imperative forms the first article of our constitution: "Human dignity shall be inviolable. To respect and protect it shall be the duty of state authority." Our democracy is based on this principle. This is the legacy of the victims of Nazi terror, especially the murdered Jews. We have accepted this obligation. . . . Our continued moral responsibility for German history led Chancellor Gerhard Schröder to take the initiative. . . .

Allow me here and now to ask forgiveness once more for the crimes of the Nazis on behalf of the younger generations of Germans who know that with our heritage we have taken on the obligation to remember our past. . . . They know, and everyone else should be aware of this too: "legal closure" by no means implies "moral closure", let alone drawing a line under the past, either historically or morally. The moral responsibility will continue and will shape German politics both at home and abroad. Germany is aware of its particular historical obligation towards the right of existence and the security of the State of Israel. This obligation cannot be diminished and will continue to shape the unique character of our relations with Israel. . . .

Our responsibility for our history must also stand the very practical test of creating an open, tolerant country in an integrated Europe. We will therefore stand up firmly against all forms of anti-Semitism, racism and xenophobia. I would like to state very clearly that as long as synagogues in Germany have to be protected by the police, as long as people are attacked because of their religion, origin or the color of their skin, we must not ease up in our fight against those who are shaking the very foundations of our democracy and society. . . .

At the beginning of the new century, the "never again", the lesson to be learned from our history, remains the basic principle in German politics and policies: within our country, in Europe, towards Israel and the Jewish communities, in our commitment to peace and respect for human rights around the world. That is the moral obligation, as well as the firm political will, of the generation of those who must shoulder responsibility for the heavy burden of German history.

Keep memories alive and assume responsibility—that will also be our message to our children and grandchildren. As it says in Psalm 78:
"Was wir hörten und erfuhren,
was uns die Väter erzählten,
das wollen wir unseren Kindern nicht verbergen,
sondern dem kommenden Geschlecht erzählen . . . "

"Things we have heard and known,
things that our fathers told us.
We will not keep them from our children;
we will tell the next generation. . . . "

DOCUMENT 49

THE EURO: A NEW EUROPEAN CURRENCY, 2000*

As part of their efforts to increase economic integration and cooperation, the member states of the European Union officially agreed to establish a common currency, and plans proceeded during the decade of the 1990s for its partial introduction in 1999. The transition period continued from 1999 to early 2002, when the new currency, designated as the "euro," became the common currency for twelve of the fifteen EU states: Austria, Belgium, Finland, France, Germany, Greece, Ireland, Italy, Luxembourg, Netherlands, Portugal, and Spain. The following is a speech delivered by Willem Duisenberg of the Netherlands, the President of the European Central Bank, on

* By permission of the European Central Bank.

December 19, 2000. The ECB regulates the broad monetary and fiscal policies of the EU, and its decisions greatly affect the economic conditions of the member states. His comments provide a helpful explanation and assessment of the objectives and effects of the new monetary system.

γ   γ   γ

Ladies and gentlemen, distinguished guests. May I first say that it is an honour to be invited to say a few words to you this evening about Europe's new single currency, the euro. I have to admit that one would not normally think of a currency as being a particularly likely or interesting subject for a dinner speech. For the euro, however, I think I am correct in saying that this is not the case. Indeed, the euro is a currency quite unlike any other. It is not a national currency. Instead it is a supra-national currency created by a monetary union of 11, soon to be 12, sovereign member states creating the second largest monetary area in the world. It is also a very new currency, still less than two years old. It does not yet circulate in the form of banknotes and coins. Not surprisingly, therefore, the euro does indeed attract a great deal of public attention.

It is notable, however, that different observers seem to perceive the euro in very different ways. Some focus their attention almost exclusively on the exchange rate, overlooking the fact that the ECB's principal aim is to maintain price stability and not a fixed exchange rate. Others seem to consider the euro purely in terms of a political or economic experiment. They fail to notice that it is already a fully functioning single currency. This only deserves to convince me that, even two years after its introduction, there is still a need for the euro to be explained to the public at large. Therefore, I very much welcome this opportunity to say a few quite general words to you about what the euro is, how it works, and what it means, both for the euro area and for the world at large.

Let me first say that one should never try to understand Europe's new currency in isolation or as a currency which was merely introduced on 1 January 1999. In fact, the euro is just one, albeit an important, part of the process of creating an economic as well as a monetary union in Europe. This process began already a decade ago. Similarly, this "Economic and Monetary Union" is itself part of a much broader process of European economic and political integration. Therefore, in order truly to understand the euro one should in fact consider it first in the context of the European integration process that began already five decades ago.

From the beginning, the purpose of this process was to bring the countries of Europe and their economies closer together and, in so doing, create an area of peace, prosperity and stability. I suppose these motivations are by no means dissimilar to those which lie behind the various other regional links which have since been formed in other parts of the world, including here in Asia. The European experience in working towards this goal has been one of gradual progress, even though with numerous ups and downs. Nonetheless, the main objective remained ever intact. As economic integration progressed further and further, as we overcame ever more subtle barriers to trade, it became increasingly apparent that one substantial barrier to the creation of a truly pan-European economy remained. I refer of course to the persistence of exchange rate fluctuations which resulted from the existence of separate national currencies governed by independent monetary policies.

In short, European policy-makers had to face up to the fact that, over extended periods of time, you cannot simultaneously maintain free trade, unrestricted capital movements, fixed exchange rates and independent monetary policies. A choice had to be made and ultimately the time arrived when most European countries deemed it more advantageous to firm up the European "Single Market" than to maintain their national currencies. I should add that, beyond this more fundamental motivation, there were other important developments which probably influenced the decision to adopt a common currency. The end of the Cold War set new political parameters for the integration of Western Europe. Regional integration and the creation of a large economic area have also come to be seen as even more necessary in order to prosper in an increasingly globalised world economy.

From the point of view of a central banker, the evolving consensus as to the appropriate role of monetary policy and of a central bank was particularly important in laying the foundation for a viable single currency. Moreover, an increasing awareness that using monetary policy directly to stimulate growth and employment was not working and was even proving counterproductive, might have strengthened the perception that, in an already deeply integrated Europe, there was little to lose from giving up autonomous monetary policies. By contrast, a good deal could be gained by removing exchange rate fluctuations and by establishing an independent European Central Bank with a clear objective to maintain price stability.

But the evolving consensus to which I refer did not just apply to the field of monetary policy. Nor would it be correct to say that consensus on the objective of monetary policy is sufficient for the creation of a successful monetary union. The euro becoming a reality also depended on the consensus which evolved of the need for sound economic policies more generally. This made it possible for all of the countries which have now adopted the euro to develop and agree on the overall economic framework needed to complement and support a monetary union. Like the process of European integration itself, a framework for co-ordinating economic policies has developed gradually and over a considerable period of time. The result is a flexible framework in which national polices are appropriately co-ordinated rather than centralised. And this is indeed quite appropriate. In a monetary union it is even more necessary than before for economic policies to take national differences into account.

On the other hand, we do see a need to ensure that national policies take into account the shared responsibility of participation in the single currency. That is why, in the area of fiscal policy, co-ordination does take quite a strong form with national policies being subject to binding rules. In this context, governments have committed themselves to what is called the Pact for Stability and Growth in order to reduce government deficits to close to balance or even to create surpluses in their budgets. And indeed over the past years, government finance positions in Europe have improved remarkably. In other policy areas, however, the countries of the euro area continued to co-ordinate their policies in more subtle ways. They exchange ideas and information, they agree [on] general guidelines and recommendations, and they regularly monitor and share assessment of each others' policies. In this way, economic co-ordination, in all its various forms, promotes and, where necessary, ensures that national policies are appropriate and consistent with participation in the single currency. In strictly legal terms the euro may be a "currency without a state". In practice, like any other currency, it is embedded in a well-developed and comprehensive economic policy framework.

Of course, the one area of policy which is now completely centralised is monetary policy. The countries which have adopted the euro now share a common currency, a single exchange rate and a single monetary policy. The responsibility for conducting this policy has been given to the ECB/Eurosystem, with a clear mandate to maintain price stability. Like the Federal Reserve System in the United States, Europe's central bank is organised as a federal system. In the centre is the ECB, based in Frankfurt am Main, Germany. The national central banks (NCBs) of the countries which have adopted the euro are also part of what we call the Eurosystem. Monetary policy decisions are made by the Governing Council of the ECB. This Council comprises the six members of the ECB's Executive Board and the Governors or Presidents of the NCBs of the countries which have adopted the euro. Decisions are made on a one person/one vote basis. This reflects the fact that they always have to be made in the interest of the euro area as a whole. Therefore, members of the Governing Council do not represent their country or even their NCB. They have been appointed in a personal capacity. This mandate is to maintain price stability in the euro area as a whole. The Eurosystem is an independent entity. This is enshrined in the Treaty establishing the European Community, which as been ratified by all the 15 Member States of the European Union.

And let me just say that I am quite proud of our achievements so far. The ECB's monetary policy and its strategy have worked well, in spite of the initial uncertainties associated with the changeover to the single currency. Price stability is being maintained, even if recent price increases have temporarily exceeded our target, mainly as a result of the almost tripling of oil prices. Moreover, the markets seem to have confidence in the ECB and its policies, as is shown by the level of long-term interest rates. In the euro area, these have remained persistently at or below US levels.

But let me move on, since the euro also has implications extending well beyond the euro area which I should also briefly touch upon. As I mentioned earlier, the euro is the currency of the world's second largest monetary area. The euro/dollar foreign exchange market is the largest in the world and around 40% of international debt securities issued over the past two years have been in euro. The euro is already an international currency, second only to the US dollar, and businesses and investors around the world need to take this into account. In this regard, however, let me just say that some of the speculation about the international role of the euro, and especially the suggestion made by some that the euro would soon rival the dollar, has not been particularly helpful. I prefer to refrain from making such predictions. Rather, I believe that the attractiveness of a currency depends crucially on the underlying policies for economic growth in the country, or countries, concerned.

What I can say with confidence, is that the euro is playing and will continue to play a role in offering new and good investment opportunities, including for investors based outside the euro area. In this regard, the euro is already acting as a catalyst for the development of a fully integrated European capital market. This market will be more efficient and more liquid than the segmented, national markets which preceded it. Ultimately, however, and I repeat, the extent to which this translates into actual inward investment will depend on the market's perception of economic policies and growth potential in the euro area.

And this brings me to another important role for the euro, namely, it acts as a catalyst for economic reform. Among other things, the adoption of a single currency means that euro area governments no longer have national currencies which they can devalue in times of need to protect inefficient industries. Instead, other ways have to be found to maintain competitiveness, both within the euro area and internationally. I believe it is no coincidence that policy-makers across Europe are now focusing more than ever before on how to overcome the economic rigidities which, in recent years, have tended to hold Europe back in terms of economic growth. Indeed, I would not even be that surprised if, looking back some years from now, it is as a catalyst for reform that the euro will be deemed to have had its most profound effect.

I should add that a lot of progress has already been made. In addition to low inflation, economic growth in the euro area is higher than it has been for a decade and unemployment is on a clear downward trend. Budgets have been consolidated and structural reforms are under way. If this development continues, I am confident that the euro has a very promising future.

In the meantime, however, another "euro changeover" will occur. One which, for ordinary euro area citizens, will not only have a profound but also an immediate and clearly perceptible impact on their daily lives. I refer to the introduction, in a year's time from now, of euro banknotes and coins. As any of you who have travelled to the euro area recently will have noticed, even though our currency is now officially the euro, we are still continuing to use our national banknotes and coins for the time being. In just over a year, however, all this will change. You will then be able to travel some 3,000 kilometers or so from Lapland in the north of Finland to Andalucia in the south of Spain without needing to visit a single *bureau de change*. No doubt, this is one implication of the single currency that at least the more mobile citizens of the euro area, myself included, as well as visitors from abroad, will very much appreciate.

DOCUMENT 50

CHARTER OF FUNDAMENTAL RIGHTS OF THE EUROPEAN UNION, 2000*

The following is the official English text of the Preamble and other contents of the European Union's Charter of Fundamental Rights, a document signed and proclaimed by leaders of the European Parliament, the Council, and the Commission at the European Council meeting in Nice France on December 7, 2000. A multinational European Union (EU) committee, created to write the Charter of Fundamental Rights, was composed of 15 representatives of the Heads of State or Government of the 15 member states of the European Union, 30 representatives of the 15 national parliaments, 16 representatives of the European Parliament, and 1 representative of the European Commission. The committee held its first meeting in December 1999 and approved the draft on October 2, 2000. The document represents the extensive range of principles, legal standards, and social objectives to be provided within democratic systems in general and the EU in particular. Each article number in the Charter contains descriptions and clarifications under the specific heading. At least one of these explanations for each article is included here. Those wishing the complete text may access the document at http://www.europarl.eu.int/charter.

γ   γ   γ

* Office for Official Publications of the European Comunities.

PREAMBLE:

The peoples of Europe, in creating an ever closer union among them, are resolved to share a peaceful future based on common values.

Conscious of its spiritual and moral heritage, the Union is founded on the indivisible, universal values of human dignity, freedom, equality and solidarity; it is based on the principles of democracy and the rule of law. It places the individual at the heart of its activities, by establishing the citizenship of the Union and by creating an area of freedom, security and justice.

The Union contributes to the preservation and to the development of these common values while respecting the diversity of the cultures and traditions of the peoples of Europe as well as the national identities of the Member States, and the organisation of their public authorities at national, regional and local levels; it seeks to promote balanced and sustainable development and ensures free movement of persons, goods, services and capital, and the freedom of establishment.

To this end, it is necessary to strengthen the protection of fundamental rights in the light of changes in society, social progress and scientific and technological developments by making those rights more visible in a Charter.

The Charter reaffirms, with due regard for the powers and tasks of the Community and the Union and the principle of subsidiarity, the rights as they result, in particular, from the constitutional traditions and international obligations common to the Member States, the Treaty on European Union, the Community Treaties, the European Convention for the Protection of Human Rights and Fundamental Freedoms, the Social Charters adopted by the Community and by the Council of Europe and the case-law of the Court of Justice of the European Communities and of the European Court of Human Rights.

Enjoyment of these rights entails responsibilities and duties with regard to other persons, to the human community and to future generations.

The Union therefore recognises the rights, freedoms and principles set out hereafter.

DIGNITY:

Article 1. Human Dignity. Human dignity is inviolable. It must be respected and protected.

Article 2. Right to life. Everyone has the right to life. No one shall be condemned to the death penalty, or executed.

Article 3. Right to the integrity of the person. Everyone has the right to respect for his or her physical and mental integrity.

Article 4. Prohibition of torture and inhuman or degrading treatment or punishment. No one shall be subjected to torture or to inhuman or degrading treatment or punishment.

Article 5. Prohibition of slavery and forced labour. No one shall be held in slavery or servitude. No one shall be required to perform forced or compulsory labour.

FREEDOMS:

Article 6. Right to liberty and security. Everyone has the right to liberty and security of person.

Article 7. Respect of private and family life. Everyone has the right to respect for his or her private and family life, home and communications.

Article 8. Protection of personal data. Everyone has the right to the protection of personal data concerning him or her. Such data must be processed fairly for specified purposes and on the basis of the consent of the person concerned or some other legitimate basis laid down by law. Everyone has the right of access to data which has been collected concerning him or her, and the right to have it rectified.

Article 9. Right to marry and right to found a family. The right to marry and the right to found a family shall be guaranteed in accordance with the national laws governing the exercise of these rights.

Article 10. Freedom of thought, conscience and religion. Everyone has the right to freedom of thought, conscience and religion. This right includes freedom to change religion or belief and freedom, either alone or in community with others and in public or in private, to manifest religion or belief, in worship, teaching, practice and observance.

Article 11. Freedom of expression and information. Everyone has the right to freedom of expression. This right shall include freedom to hold opinions and to receive and impart information and ideas without interference by public authority and regardless of frontiers. The freedom and pluralism of the media shall be respected.

Article 12. Freedom of assembly and of association. Everyone has the right to freedom of peaceful assembly and to freedom of association at all levels, in particular in political, trade union and civic matters, which implies the right of everyone to form and to join trade unions for the protection of his or her interests. Political parties at Union level contribute to expressing the political will of the citizens of the Union.

Article 13. Freedom of the arts and sciences. The arts and scientific research shall be free of constraint. Academic freedom shall be respected.

Article 14. Right to education. Everyone has the right to education and to have access to vocational and continuing training. This right includes the possibility to receive free compulsory education.

Article 15. Freedom to choose an occupation and right to engage in work. Everyone has the right to engage in work and to pursue a freely chosen or accepted occupation. Every citizen of the Union has the freedom to seek employment to work, to exercise the right of establishment and to provide services in any Member State. Nationals of third countries who are authorised to work in the territories of the Member States are entitled to working conditions equivalent to those of citizens of the Union.

Article 16. Freedom to conduct a business. The freedom to conduct a business in accordance with Community law and national laws and practices is recognised.

Article 17. Right to property. Everyone has the right to own, use, dispose of and bequeath his or her lawfully acquired possessions. No one may be deprived of his or her possessions, except in the public interest and in the cases and under the conditions provided for by law, subject to fair compensation being paid in good time for their loss. The use of property may be regulated by law in so far as is necessary for the general interest.

Article 18. Right to asylum. The right to asylum shall be guaranteed with due respect for the rules of the Geneva Convention of 28 July 1951 and the Protocol of 31 January 1967 relating to the status of refugees and in accordance with the Treaty establishing the European Community.

Article 19. Protection in the event of removal, expulsion or extradition. Collective expulsions are prohibited. No one may be removed, expelled or extradited to a State where there is a serious risk that he or she would be subjected to the death penalty, torture or other inhuman or degrading treatment or punishment.

EQUALITY:
Article 20. Equality before the law. Everyone is equal before the law.

Article 21. Non-discrimination. Any discrimination based on any ground such as sex, race, colour, ethnic or social origin, genetic features, languages, religion or belief, political or any other opinion, membership of a national minority, property, birth, disability, age or sexual orientation shall be prohibited.

Article 22. Cultural, religious and linguistic diversity. The Union shall respect cultural, religious and linguistic diversity.

Article 23. Equality between men and women. Equality between men and women must be ensured in all areas, including employment, work and pay. The principle of equality shall not prevent the maintenance or adoption of measures providing for specific advantages in favour of the under-represented sex.

Article 24. The rights of the child. Children shall have the right to such protection and care as is necessary for their well-being. They may express their views freely. Such views shall be taken into consideration on matters which concern them in accordance with their age and maturity.

In all actions relating to children, whether taken by public authorities or private institutions, the child's best interests must be a primary consideration.

Article 25. The rights of the elderly. The Union recognises and respects the rights of the elderly to lead a life of dignity and independence and to participate in social and cultural life.

Article 26. Integration of persons with disabilities. The Union recognises and respects the right of persons with disabilities to benefit from measures designed to ensure their independence, social and occupational integration and participation in the life of the community.

SOLIDARITY:

Article 27. Workers' right to information and consultation within the undertaking. Workers or their representatives must, at the appropriate levels, be guaranteed information and consultation in good time in the cases and under the conditions provided for by Community law and national laws and practices.

Article 28. Right of collective bargaining and action. Workers and employers, or their respective organisations, have, in accordance with Community law and national laws and practices the right to negotiate and conclude collective agreements at the appropriate levels and, in cases of conflicts of interest, to take collective action to defend their interests. include strike action.

Article 29. Right of access to placement services. Everyone has the right of access to a free placement service.

Article 30. Protection in the event of unjustified dismissal. Every worker has the right of protection against unjustified dismissal, in accordance with Community law and national laws and practice.

Article 31. Fair and just working conditions. Every worker has the right to working conditions with respect his or her health, safety and dignity. Every worker has the right to limitation of maximum working hours, to daily and weekly rest periods and to an annual period of paid leave.

Article 32. Prohibition of child labour and protection of young children at work. The employment of children is prohibited. The minimum age of admission to employment may not be lower than the minimum school-leaving age, without prejudice to such rules as may be more favourable to young people and except for limited derogations. Young people admitted to work must have working conditions appropriate to their age and be protected against economic exploitation and any work likely to harm their safety, health or physical, mental, moral or social development or to interfere with their education.

Article 33. Family and professional life. The family shall enjoy legal, economic and social protection. To reconcile family and professional life, everyone shall have the right to protection from dismissal for a reason connected with maternity and the right to paid maternity leave and to parental leave following the birth or adoption of a child.

Article 34. Social security and social assistance. The Union recognises and respects the entitlement to social security benefits and social services providing protection in cases such as maternity, illness, industrial accidents, dependency or old age, and in the case of loss of employment, in accordance with the rules laid down by Community law and national laws and practices. Everyone residing and moving legally within the European Union is entitled to social security benefits and social advantages in accordance with Community law and national law and practices.

Article 35. Health care. Everyone has the right of access to preventive health care and the right to benefit from medical treatment under the conditions established by national laws and practices. A high level of human health protection shall be ensured in the definition and implementation of all Union policies and activities.

Article 36. Access to services of general economic interest. The Union recognises and respects access to services of general economic interest as provided for in national laws and practices, in accordance with the Treaty establishing the European Community, in order to promote the social and territorial cohesion of the Union.

Article 37. Environmental protection. A high level of environmental protection and the improvement of the quality of the environment must be integrated into the policies of the Union and ensured in accordance with the principle of sustainable development.

Article 38. Consumer protection. Union policies shall ensure a high level of consumer protection.

CITIZENS' RIGHTS:

Article 39. Right to vote and to stand as a candidate at elections to the European Parliament. Every citizen of the Union has the right to vote and to stand as a candidate at elections to the European Parliament in the Member State in which he or she resides, under the same conditions as nationals of that State. Members of the European Parliament shall be elected by direct universal suffrage in a free and secret ballot.

Article 40. Right to vote and to stand as a candidate at municipal elections. Every citizen of the Union has the right to vote and to stand as a candidate at municipal elections in the Member State in which he or she resides under the same conditions as nationals of that State.

Article 41. Right to good administration. Every person has the right to have his or her affairs handled impartially, fairly and within a reasonable time by the institutions and bodies of the Union.

Article 42. Right of access to documents. Any citizen of the Union, and any natural or legal person residing or having its registered office in a Member State, has a right of access to European Parliament, Council and Commission documents.

Article 43. Ombudsman. Any citizen of the Union and any natural or legal person residing or having its registered office in a Member State has the right to refer to the Ombudsman of the Union cases of maladministration in the activities of the Community institutions or bodies, with the exception of the Court of Justice and the Court of First Instance acting in their judicial role.

Article 44. Right to petition. Any citizen of the Union and any natural or legal person residing or having its registered office in a Member State has the right to petition the European Parliament.

Article 45. Freedom of movement and of residence. Every citizen of the Union has the right to move and reside freely within the territory of the Member States. Freedom of movement and residence may be granted, in accordance with the Treaty establishing the European Community, to nationals of third countries legally resident in the territory of a Member State.

Article 46. Diplomatic and consular protection. Every citizen of the Union shall, in the territory of a third country in which the Member State of which he or she is a national is not represented, be entitled to protection by the diplomatic or consular authorities of any Member State, on the same conditions as the nationals of that Member State.

JUSTICE:
Article 47. Right to an effective remedy and to a fair trial. Everyone whose rights and freedoms guaranteed by the law of the Union are violated has the right to an effective remedy before a tribunal in compliance with the conditions laid down in this article. Everyone is entitled to a fair and public hearing within a reasonable time by an independent and impartial tribunal previously established by law. Everyone shall have the possibility of being advised, defended and represented. Legal aid shall be made available to those who lack sufficient resources in so far as such aid is necessary to ensure effective access to justice.

Article 48. Presumption of innocence and right of defence. Everyone who has been charged shall be presumed innocent until proved guilty according to law. Respect for the rights of the defence of anyone who has been charged shall be guaranteed.

Article 49. Principles of legality and proportionality of criminal offences and penalties. No one shall be held guilty of any criminal offence on account of any act or omission which did not constitute a criminal offence under national law or international law at the time when it was committed. Nor shall a heavier penalty be imposed than that which was applicable at the time the criminal offence was committed. If, subsequent to the commission of a criminal offence, the law provides for a lighter penalty, that penalty shall be applicable. The severity of penalties must not be disproportionate to the criminal offence.

Article 50. Right not to be tried or punished twice in criminal proceedings for the same criminal offence. No one shall be liable to be tried or punished again in criminal proceedings for an offence for which he or she has already been finally acquitted or convicted within the Union in accordance with the law.

GENERAL PROVISIONS:

Article 51. Scope. The provisions of this Charter are addressed to the institutions and bodies of the Union with due regard for the principle of subsidiarity and to the Member States only when they are implementing Union law. They shall therefore respect the rights, observe the principles and promote the application thereof in accordance with their respective powers.

Article 52. Scope of guaranteed rights. Any limitation on the exercise of the rights and freedoms recognised by this Charter must be provided for by laws and respect the essence of those rights and freedoms. Subject to the principles of proportionality, limitations may be made only if they are necessary and genuinely meet objectives of general interests recognised by the Union or the need to protect the rights and freedoms of others.

Article 53. Level of protection. Nothing in this Charter shall be interpreted as restricting or adversely affecting human rights and fundamental freedoms as recognised, in their respective fields of application, by Union law and international law and by international agreements in which the Union, the Community or all the Member States are party, including the European Convention for the Protection of Human Rights and Fundamental Freedoms, and by the Member States' constitutions.

Article 54. Prohibition of abuse of rights. Nothing in this Charter shall be interpreted as implying any right to engage in any activity or to perform any act aimed at the destruction of any of the rights and freedoms recognized in this Charter or at their limitation to a greater extent than is provided for herein.

ABOUT THE AUTHOR

Taylor Stults is the coauthor of a widely used textbook and author of numerous articles in European and Russian history. He is Emeritus Professor of History at Muskingum College, where he taught from 1962 to 2001. His research interests include NATO and the Cold War era. His undergraduate degree is from Antioch College, and his M.A. and Ph.D. are from the University of Missouri. Dr. Stults is a former President of the Ohio Academy of History and received its Distinguished Service Award in 1996.